CHILD SOLDIERS: VICTIMS AND AGGRESSORS

A Problematic for Public Safety in Haiti

PART I: 550 BC TO AD 2006

ALFRED REYNOLDS

Order this book online at www.trafford.com
or email orders@trafford.com

Most Trafford titles are also available at major online book retailers.

Print information available on the last page.

ISBN: 978-1-6987-1097-6 (sc)
ISBN: 978-1-6987-1099-0 (hc)
ISBN: 978-1-6987-1098-3 (e)

Library of Congress Control Number: 2022902281

Trafford rev. 02/04/2022

www.trafford.com
North America & international
toll-free: 844-688-6899 (USA & Canada)
fax: 812 355 4082

Misnaming things is to add to the misfortune of the world!
—Albert Camus

This book is dedicated to my wife, Judith Wagnac
. . . and to my children, Djenaba, Mark,
Justin, Nehemaya, Izhar, and Zahra.

My sincere thanks to

Paule Goulet, a wonderful woman. Her support and advice have helped me stay strong in difficult moments during my stay in Quebec;

my research director, Prof. Julie Desrosiers. Her multiple comments have allowed me to work over my approaches in writing this essay;

the following law professors: Georges Azzaria, Christian Brunelle, Olivier Delas, Denis Lemieux, Bjarne Melkevik, Alain Prujiner, Dominic Roux, and Pierre Rainville, for their expertise in legal teaching and their intellectual support while I was a graduate student at Université Laval;

the teaching team at the Feminist University (summer 2006, Université Laval), for their various sociopolitico-economic and legal approaches on the problems that are confronting women and minorities who are living in Quebec and the world in general;

and, finally, the marvelous team from the International Bureau for Children's Rights (IBCR), who has given me an internship opportunity in Montreal to better understand the situation of children throughout the world.

CONTENTS

Foreword... xv

About The Author xix

Abbreviations And Acronyms.. xxiii

Introduction.. xxvii

Part I The Child and His Status of "Soldier" in Armed Conflicts

Chapter 1   The Child Soldier in The New Millennium.................. 1

1.1 Brief history of the "child soldier" 1

1.2 The different approaches of recruitment 4

1.2.1 The recruitment by force 5

1.2.2 The voluntary recruitment... 6

1.3 The causes for children recruitment................................ 7

1.3.1 From the interest of recruiters or warlords 8

1.3.2 From the vulnerability of recruits or
         future child soldiers... 8

1.4 The effects of children recruitment............................... 10

1.4.1 The immediate effects... 10

1.4.2 The long-term effects... 11

Chapter 2   The Paradoxical Status of Child Soldiers:
             Victims and Aggressors...................................... 13

2.1 The concept of "child victim" 13

2.2 The concept of "child aggressor" 14

2.3 The consequences of the paradoxical status of
       child soldier 15

2.3.1 An opportunity for the systemic
      recruitment of children 19

2.3.1.1 Impunity for recruiters or warlords 21

2.3.1.2 Standardization of children recruitment 24

2.3.1.3 Utilization and implication of children in
        armed conflicts 26

2.3.2 The systematic delinquency of children.................... 29

2.3.2.1 Implication of children in acts of delinquency......... 31

2.3.2.2 Impunity for child soldiers 33

Part II The Indecisiveness of International Law regarding the Legal Status of Child Soldiers

Chapter 3   The Role of International Law in the Protection
             of the Rights of the Child 39

3.1 The child and the rules of international
    humanitarian law 39

3.1.1 Age limit for the conscription of the child soldier 40

3.1.2 Serious offenses: between reconciliation and
      legal prosecutions 42

3.2 The child and the international
    rules of human rights 43

3.2.1 The social and political rights of the child................. 43

3.2.2 The rights and freedom of the child at work 46

Chapter 4   International Law and the
             Paradoxical Status of Child Soldiers............................ 49

4.1 The child soldier and the legal
    system of juvenile delinquency..................................... 50

4.1.1 The concept of "juvenile delinquency"...................... 51

4.1.2 The insurmountable dangers to the
        "socialization process"................................. 53

4.2 The child soldier and the weaknesses of
     international conventions............................. 54

4.2.1 The status of the child soldier in drafting of
        conventions 56

4.2.2 The status of the child soldier in the
        acceptance of conventions ....:........... 59

4.3 The paradoxical status of the child
     soldier during armed conflicts 63

4.3.1 The child soldier or child victim 64

4.3.2 The victims of child soldiers............................. 66

4.3.3 The child soldier or child aggressor....................... 67

4.3.4 The aggressors of child soldiers 68

4.4 The nonparadoxical status of the child soldier
     following armed conflicts 69

4.4.1 The child soldiers: victims or aggressors................. 70

4.4.2 The aggressors: child soldiers and warlords............... 72

Part III The International Community's Responses to Armed Conflicts and Their Susceptibility to Bring Antagonistic Solutions to the Problems of Child Soldiers: The Case of Haiti

Chapter 5   Genesis and Evolution of the "Civil War" in
            Haiti: An Open Debate 81

5.1 The violence in Haiti.................................... 84

5.2 The armed actors in the conflict.................... 93

5.2.1 The Haitian armed forces and the
        international and multinational forces 94

5.2.2 The political parties and armed movements............. 100

Chapter 6   The Recent Evolution of the Armed Conflict........... 109

  6.1 Narco-trafficking, armed groups, and conflict........... 109

  6.2 Intensification and internationalization.......................112

  6.3 The political approach of the UN without any
      regard for a legal solution 114

  6.4 The DDR programs and the vigilante groups............. 117

  6.4.1 The revolutionary period 118

  6.4.2 The American occupation period............................ 120

  6.4.3 The period of "constitutional return" to order........ 122

  6.4.4 The first period of occupation
        by multinational forces.. 123

  6.4.5 The second period of occupation by
        multinational forces... 124

Conclusion 131
Appendix 137
Bibliography..151

FOREWORD

Child soldiers are a special legal category of people. There are legal provisions that govern specific aspects of their situation. Some aspects remain still insufficiently explored, including their paradoxical status of victim and aggressor in international law. Alfred Reynolds's book is timely raising this issue.

The thesis of this book demonstrates the fluctuating nature of the child soldier. Often considered a victim, he is treated as such by the law. He is incapable and therefore irresponsible to the international court. At the same time, however, that victim turns into an aggressor, and it is here that international law demonstrates its inconsistency by not subjugating him from the same justice. This particular problem highlights the merit of the author who has been able to show the inconsistencies of international law on this dual nature. Here, we have an original work that goes on more than one issue against the grain of certain widespread ideas about the nature of the child soldier and the legal regime should be applied to them. To shed some light on this issue, Alfred Reynolds brings us back to the origins of the phenomenon. He could settle for a description of this phenomenon, but he goes far beyond, highlighting the underlying reasons and justifications. He does not stop in his work to stress the predominance of international law on this subject. Therefore, one becomes aware that the recruitment of child soldiers can also be done solely because of the legal irresponsibility of this category of person under international law. Finally, reading the work of Alfred Reynolds raises the question whether international law does not encourage the phenomenon of child soldiers. Supposed to adjust at first, the law will appear in a new light as a facilitator of abnormalities. One gets to be convinced of the need to rethink the nature of the protection that international law gives to such persons.

The thought of the author goes further than that. This is not a quest to challenge the international regulatory provisions to protect children. More than that, on one side, it is to bring into the open the effects of the international protection of the rights of others who are victims of child soldiers, the latter also becoming aggressors under guaranteed impunity. On the other side, it is to consider a better way for national courts to have the monopoly to suppress the actions of those children. Here, the author shows the incongruities of national criminal systems and their inadequacy to the reality of the situation they need to resolve.

In short, the work of Alfred Reynolds leads us to ask ourselves how international law can help solve the problem of child soldiers. What might be the direction of international action on this issue? It is not enough to simply enact their impunity and to leave the national legal systems to deal with it. Alfred Reynolds provides a new framework for thinking about the focus of international action. He argues for a rethinking of international law on the suppression of recruitment of child soldiers. Finally, the novelty of this book is that it presents a compelling responsibility of the international community on the issue of child soldiers. Key stakeholders such as international organizations and civil society are blacklisted for the lack of means to contribute to solving this problem. The author argues that the politicization of this issue by the United Nations (UN) in defiance of a legal solution and, later, its resignation do not seem likely to change this situation.

Reading the work of Alfred Reynolds leads almost inevitably to embrace his proposals. If some of his questions may, at first glance, appear somewhat Byzantine, he almost always ends up convincing the interest of the problem he raises and the accuracy of the solution he advocates. In this case, the action of the international community could address the suppression of all behaviors that are the source of the phenomenon of child soldiers. This book happens to persuade us of the need to rethink the nature of international action, including the international legal action, regarding the issue of child soldiers.

Edouard Dieudonné Onguene Onana

Doctor of International Law

ABOUT THE AUTHOR

Alfred Reynolds was born in Port-au-Prince where he worked as a reporter for Radio Plus. In September 1989, he almost got killed by a vigilante group. In fact, the present political situation of his native country does not really surprise the author. Like other countries in Africa, the Middle East, and Latin America that are experiencing firsthand democratic changes, Haiti—since February 1986—is the scene of acts of violence that are well planned and executed by both sides of the political spectrum. However, what has changed from 1986 to 2006 is the focus of the author. One can ask how the problems of child soldiers are real in Haiti considering the program of Disarmament, Demobilization, and Reintegration (DDR) of the United Nations Stabilization Mission in Haiti (MINUSTAH). Further, one can wonder where Haiti stands in terms of ratification of international instruments to protect the rights of the child. The author decides to focus on the topic of "child soldiers" because of the use of children in armed conflicts around the world, in countries such as Haiti, where the subject is taboo.

With his years of professional experiences and his educational background, Alfred is trying to answer all the above questions in the third chapter of this essay, which is based on his academic research at University Laval, School of Law, where he got his master of laws (LLM) in International and Transnational Laws. In fact, in 2006, he landed a position in Montreal, Quebec (Canada), to work for the International Bureau for Children Rights (IBCR), where he acquired most of his expertise by targeting countries in North Africa while working on his law degree. Alfred has contributed to the publication of the annual IBCR's report in 2007 and has published several articles and online journal reviews and blogs concerning the criminal justice system and the necessity for a progressive reform of the Haitian legal system. Alfred is a former adjunct professor at the Community College of Vermont (CCV) in Saint Albans, Vermont (USA), where he specialized in criminal law, criminology, and juvenile justice. He is a former member of Vermont and Georgia Army National Guard and the US Army Reserve. He worked as an in-house counselor for children at risk in the states of Connecticut and Massachusetts. Once moving to Georgia, where he worked shortly for the Georgia Department of Juvenile Justice with the Metro Regional Youth Detention Center (RYDC), he decided to join Gwinnett County Police Department in the GCIC/NCIC Division (background unit) as a technical agency coordinator (TAC) and for Gwinnett County Juvenile Court as an intensive probation officer. Alfred graduated from Norwalk Community Technical College with an associate's degree in Criminal Justice; from Western Connecticut State University with a bachelor of science degree in Justice and Law Administration; and, finally, from different military schools with certificates in security, corrections, civil disturbance, and fatal fire investigation. Alfred is also a member of the Juvenile Court Association of Georgia (JCAG), the Gang Investigators Association of Georgia (GIAG), the Canadian Bar Association (CBA), the International Law Association, the Lawyers Without Borders, the Interdisciplinary Research Center on Family Violence and Violence on Women, and the Research Center on the Rehabilitation of Youth and Family at Risk (Quebec).

Alfred benefited from several opportunities from his law professors to hold conferences at the Cercle Europe and at the Peace Program and International Security; both are branches of the Institut Québécois des Hautes Études Internationales as well as the Summer University for Feminists (University Laval). Alfred is a juris doctor (JD) candidate. He has a graduate certificate (EdS) in Education and Leadership from the University of Georgia. Further, aside from his experiences in the legal and investigative fields, Alfred also graduated from Liberty University with a master's degree in Pastoral Ministry and Chaplaincy. He is the founder of the Haitian-American Institute for Justice and Law (HAIJL), a "think tank" and a human rights organization, which has its headquarters in Lawrenceville, Georgia (USA), where he is currently working as its executive director.

ABBREVIATIONS AND ACRONYMS

ACRC	African Charter on the Rights and the Welfare of the Child
ADF	Allied Democratic Forces
AI	Amnesty International
AU	African Union
BO	Baghdad Operation
CAID	Canadian Agency for International Development
CCPSM	Code of Crimes against the Peace and Security of Mankind
CHLR	Columbia Human Rights Law Review
CIA	Central Intelligence Agency
COE	Council of Europe
CRC	Convention on the Rights of the Child
CRC	Committee on the Rights of the Child
DEA	Drug Enforcement Administration
DDR	Disarmament, Demobilization, and Reintegration
DDRR	Disarmament, Demobilization, Reintegration, and Rehabilitation
DRC	Democratic Republic of Congo
ECOSOC	Economic and Social Council
EU	European Union
FBI	Federal Bureau of Investigation
FMNLF	Farabundo Marti National Liberation Front
GC	Geneva Convention
HCR	High Commissioner for Refugees
HRW	Human Rights Watch
ICC	International Criminal Court
ICJ	International Court of Justice
ICRC	International Committee of the Red Cross
ICHR	Inter-American Commission on Human Rights

ILO	International Labour Organization
IPCJ	International Permanent Court of Justice
IPEC	International Programme on the Elimination of Child Labour
IOW	International Organization of Workers
LRA	Lord's Resistance Army
MIFH	Multinational Interim Force in Haiti
MINUSTAH	United Nations Stabilization Mission in Haiti
MS-13	Mara Salvatrucha (Salvadorian guerilla)
NGO	nongovernmental organization
NNDHR	National Network for the Defense of Human Rights
NRA	National Resistance Army
OAS	Organization of American States
OJ	Official Journal
ONUSAL	United Nations Observer Mission in El Salvador
OPCRCAC	Optional Protocol to the Convention on the Rights of the Child on the involvement of children in armed conflict
PBS	Public Broadcasting Station
PMLA	Popular Movement for the Liberation of Angola
RGP	Riyadh Guiding Principles
RSICP	Rome Statute (International Criminal Court)
RTLM	Radio-television Libre des Mille Collines (extremist radio from Rwanda)
SC	Security Council
SLSC	Sierra Leone Special Court
TRC	Truth and Reconciliation Commission
UCP	Union of Congolese Patriots
UDHR	Universal Declaration of Human Rights
UDPF	Uganda Democratic Popular Front
UNAMIR	United Nations Assistance Mission for Rwanda
UNESCO	United Nations Educational, Scientific, and Cultural Organization

UNHCHR	United Nations High Commissioner for Human Rights
UNHCR	United Nations High Commissioner for Refugees
UNICEF	United Nations International Children's Emergency Funds
UPC	Uganda People's Congress

INTRODUCTION

Children have been used since the Stone Age to fight wild beasts and hunt for food for the survival of themselves and their clans. People in positions of power have realized quickly that children can be used as child soldiers to become either spies or assassins to kill their enemies. It was the case for the *Spartan children* who fought wars throughout 550 BC and the centuries that followed to make Sparta the most powerful military machine in ancient Greece. The recruitment of children continued in the early fourteenth century with Murad I, who—under the *devshirmke* system—drafted young boys from the peoples of conquered Christian territories. Those boys become known as the "janissaries" or "bodyguards" and "household troops."

Suleyman, the Muslim lawgiver, continued the recruitment in the Ottoman Empire throughout the sixteenth century with his army of thirty thousand child soldiers who were a true elite force, which was trained to be loyal to the sultan only. In fact, those child soldiers were called different names according to the countries they were recruited. For example, if they were not called *Spartans* or *Janissaries*, they were known as *Mamluks* (Egypt), *Cadets of La Flèche* (France), *Lebensborn* (Germany), *Bassidji* (Iran), *Erasers* (Uganda), *Kadogos* or *Vagina Snatchers* (Congo-RDC), *Mara-Salvatrucha* (El Salvador), or *Chimères* or *Kokorat* (Haiti). For the last twenty years, the number of children who are used in national and transnational armed conflicts have increased particularly in Africa, South America, and the Middle East.

In Uganda as in Pakistan, in Haiti as in Colombia, thousands of children are enlisted in armies to be involved in armed conflicts. According to Amnesty International, a member of the Coalition to

Stop the Use of Child Soldiers, "there are more than one half-million of children, less than eighteen years old, who are currently enrolled in regular and irregular armed forces, paramilitary forces and civil militia in more than 85 countries."[1] However, while most of these children have been forced to join armed groups, some of them were volunteers or willingly accepted to become child soldiers who can be at any time remorseless, easy to be brainwashed and effective killers and torturers. The Security Council believes that there are more than 250,000 children who are currently exploited and involved in armed conflicts throughout the world.[2] However, in the eyes of the world, "the problems of child soldiers are regarded as an African plague which made it possible for Africa to become the laboratory where the International Community tries to bring the first answers to several unanswered questions."[3]

According to the Cape Town Principles,[4] adopted by the United Nations Children's Funds (UNICEF), a child soldier is "any person under 18 years of age who is part of any kind of regular or irregular armed groups in any capacity, and those accompanying such groups, other than purely as family members, including girls who are recruited for sexual purposes and forced marriage." This definition was reiterated by the General Secretary of the United Nations (hereafter UN), Kofi Annan, in his report to the Security Council on children and the armed conflicts.[5] Moreover, the international rules—in

---

[1]   ACT 76/004/2003, 1 June 2003.

[2]   SC/8784, 24 July 2006.

[3]   Nairï ARZOUMANIAN and Francesca PIZZUTELLI, "Victims and executioners: questions of responsibility linked to the problem of child soldiers in Africa," (2003) 85 R.I.C.R 827.

[4]   Cape Town Principles, 27 April 1997.

[5]   S/2000/712, 19 July 2000.

particular the 4th Geneva Convention[6] of 1949, the Additional protocols (Protocol I[7] and II[8]) of 1977, the Convention on the Rights of the Child[9] and its protocol[10]—clearly proscribe the recruitment of children in armed forces or groups. Further, the recruitment and the use of children in acts of hostilities can be considered as a war crime. Indeed, the Principles of the Statute of Rome,[11] Resolution 1674[12] of the Security Council of the UN, and the Rules of Procedures[13] from the International Criminal Court (ICC) prohibit any amnesty and make obligation to any government to judge all the authors of crimes against humanity, crimes of genocide, and massive violations of international human rights.

However, despite all these rules, the international law remains ambiguous on the legal status of child soldiers and hesitates on the concepts of victims and aggressors. There is indeed a paradox in the actual definition of the child soldier: the child is both a victim and an aggressor. In protecting these children as victims, should international law keep protecting these children despite that they are also aggressors? If so, what about their victims who are killed, raped, or tortured? And, if those children should not be legally responsible for their crimes in international courts, is it wise for the international community to let those children be tried by their national courts, which mostly have a failing judicial system that cannot administer properly justice for juveniles or lack motivation to give justice to both victims and

---

[6] Articles 17 and 51 GC IV.

[7] Articles 51.1 and 77 Protocol I GC.

[8] Articles 4.3(c) and 13 Protocol II GC.

[9] Art. 38.2 CRC.

[10] Articles 2 and 4 OP-CRC-AC.

[11] Articles 6 and 8.2 (b) (xxvi) RS-ICC.

[12] SC Res. 1674, 28 April 2006.

[13] Articles 4(c) and 10 SLSC.

aggressors? This paradox, when it is ignored, can allow the child to become an easier target for recruitment, encourage the child to perpetuate its acts of delinquency, and generate serious consequences on the physical and mental states of the child. And, considering the uneasiness of the international law to view child soldiers as aggressors, it is imperative to know how the international humanitarian law and the international rules of human rights consider the problems of child soldiers when these children are at the same time victims and aggressors. Can the legal status of child soldiers be better defined in international law? In fact, who are these victims? And who are these aggressors? Can these victims also become aggressors without any regard to the law?

Our study will focus, on the one hand, on cases where the child soldier is regarded as a victim when his rights are violated by those who enlist him in armed groups; and, on the other hand, as an aggressor when the child fell into delinquency and violated the rights of those individuals who are also victims of war. Considering their experiences in armed conflicts, their psychological problems after wars, the negligence, or the refusal of the authorities to rehabilitate them, these children are left by themselves; and, to survive, they must make profitable the experiences they have acquired on the battlefields, regardless if it was with the guerrilla, armed resistances, or conventional wars. The child is now forced to live as a delinquent, thus becoming a member of the marginalized groups in the ghettos where the strongest of them rules.

Through our study, we will try to formulate principles that should be considered as well by the international organizations as government authorities in the countries where the armed conflicts emerge, for the protection of child soldiers and the administration of justice for minors. In this case, does the international law satisfy the victims, considered by many as child soldiers, and the victims of child soldiers? And, in which direction, up to what point do these victims have to be satisfied? To contribute to the efficiency of the international standards, we will examine the way in which the international rules of human rights and the international humanitarian law can approach the extent of the recruitment phenomenon, the use and the involvement of children in armed conflicts, while taking into consideration the legal status of these children who are at the same time victims and aggressors. Last, we will see that the UN program of Disarmament, Demobilization, and Reintegration (DDR) is often ineffective. In fact, this program does not offer any means of rehabilitation to these children who, for most of them, are mentally traumatized. The program tends to privilege a political approach with no regard to a legal solution and does not always contribute to the protection of the rights and freedoms and to the good administration of justice.

PART I

The Child and His Status of "Soldier" in Armed Conflicts

CHAPTER 1

The Child Soldier in The New Millennium

If the problem of child soldiers became a new international crisis during the last few decades, the extent of this problem is not a new phenomenon. It is a problem that exists for a very long time, and it will persist as long as there will be warlords, armed forces, paramilitary groups, guerrillas, and militia to start social movements and political conflicts; and, for worse, as long as there will be struggles between various social, political, and economic classes.

1.1 Brief history of the "child soldier"

Starting from the year 550 BC, the children are recruited to become soldiers. According to the Athenian writer Xenophon, in his work titled *The Republic of Lacedemonians,*[14] the entire town of Sparta has a military orientation for its youth. A commission of wise men has to go regularly from door to door to identify the babies who are beautiful, well trained, and robust. Then they take the babies from their mothers willingly or by force. Thus, the babies are given to robust nurses, who never tighten the newborns in linens so that they become quickly more corpulent and stronger. After the age of seven, the child is placed in a unit under the authority of a chief who is the oldest among them, who are regarded as a small group of the strongest fighters.[15]

---

[14] Nadeije LANEYRIE-DAGEN, *The Great Events in the History of Children,* coll. "The Memory of Humanity," Paris, Edition Larousse, 1995, p. 25.

[15] *Id.*

During the first training cycle (age seven to eleven), the child is turned over to his parents. On the second cycle (age twelve to fifteen) and third cycle (age sixteen to twenty), the child is returned to his unit and his education becomes more constraining and crueler. The child—after several trainings in running, fighting, handling of weapons (swords or javelins), and troop movements, which increase muscular endurance and the hard discipline in the battlefields—is now prepared to become a future warrior who will defend his country until his death. The boys are urged and forced to fight between themselves to test their passion in battles and to get them used to the blows. The young Spartan women, for their part, must have a firm and quite muscular body that they inherited in their childhood and during their adolescence to carry healthy and strong babies who will become also future warriors. These women or young Spartans train themselves in running and devote themselves to different physical challenges such as throwing javelins and discs. According to Xenophon, the state of Sparta wants to give to the child a moral education, but they must be pitiless. In this case, the child learns how to overcome sorrows and pains. He learns how to fight against the cold and against heat. He familiarizes himself with dirtiness. He does not eat a good meal and does not satisfy his hunger. In fact, the Spartan authorities—wanting to develop faculties of trick and street smartness in their youth—do not prevent them either from stealing. On the contrary, the clumsy robber is greatly and severely punished, not because he has committed a reprehensible offence but because he has failed in his attempt.[16]

If the history of the Spartan child soldiers goes back to hundreds of years before our era, one can see throughout the thirteenth century the exploits of the *Mamelukes* of Egypt. Very young, these Turkish children—who are between ten and fifteen years old—were bought

---

[16] *Id.*, p. 35.

in the south of Russia. In Central Asia, they became slave soldiers to save Islam against the Crusade army of Saint-Louis. In 1764, in France, one sees a military school of cadets at La Flèche College of 250 young children from eight to eleven years old, the majority of whom are sons of army officers. These children are prepared to have a military career, from a hard discipline, by physical training and handling of weapons. In 1793, Joseph Bara—a fourteen-year-old child who is enlisted in the republican army—became the child martyr of the French Revolution. During World War II, one sees the *Lebensborn* or the blond children of Hitler. These children, aged twelve to fifteen years old, are enlisted in the German army or the *Wehrmacht*, in special units such as the *Waffen-SS* and, later, take part militarily in German resistance against the foreign coalition. In 1975, several thousands of Angolan children march in the streets of Luanda, the capital of Angola, while taking part in a military parade with grenade launchers on their shoulders. Since 1980, one sees the *bassidji* or young soldier Iranians, aged thirteen to fifteen years old, who engaged themselves "voluntarily" in the army, with the assent of their parents, to participate in the war with Iraq. When these children become child soldiers within an armed force, they can play various functions: cook, carrier, messenger, and many others. The child is also used as a scout or a guide to remove mines to cut through the path for his war companions. Often, the child loses a limb or even loses his life. However, there are exceptional cases where the child—once becoming a leader following years of war experience in regular armed forces or in the guerrilla—is actively involved in conflicts by giving orders to plan, prepare, start, or simply attack another armed group or a population.

During these wars, multiple atrocities are invariably made by those attackers, whether they are children or adults. According to the United Nations, in 1994, between 250,000 and 500,000 women were raped in ninety days during the genocide in Rwanda. Among the women who survived the genocide, 80 percent were raped and more than half of them were infected by the AIDS virus. According to Mrs. Iulia Motoc, in her report on the situation of human rights in the Democratic Republic of Congo (DRC), "the situation of women and children is degraded continuously because of the continuation of the conflicts and the climate of terror by the rebellious armed groups in the territory."[17] In addition, "the age of the rapists tends to lower with the extent of recruitment of child soldiers in African wars," while five years old girls and eighty years old women are raped with an extraordinary brutality particularly when the attackers introduce weapons inside their victims or "into their vagina or mutilating them with knives or razor blades."[18] In fact, the story of the Spartans and the Mamelukes show that the recruitment of child soldiers is very important for those who like to make war. The various approaches of recruitment, especially in the new millennium, require a greater debate when these recruitments are made by force or voluntarily and when the children who are recruited will be used in armed conflicts.

1.2 The different approaches of recruitment

The recruitment of new soldiers is important to maintain an armed force. Thus, the recruiters will use the most effective way to recruit young people, and the quantitative results always take precedence over the qualitative requirements in time of war. For example, in conventional armed forces, the military recruiters from Western countries benefit often from the needs of young people, members of the minorities, and the middle class who are going to college or are still in college, to offer them enticing subsidies: the possibilities to go to college and many other benefits. We are

---

[17] A/57/437, 26 September 2002.

[18] HUMAN RIGHTS WATCH, *War within War: Sexual Violence Against Women and Girls in Eastern Congo*, Brussels, Human Rights Watch, 2002, p. 3.

interested, as for us, in children who are living in countries where there are armed conflicts and no conventional armed forces. In these places, young children are increasingly being recruited to take part in armed conflicts, whether their participation in those conflicts are done in a direct or indirect way. However, indirectly, they become sexual messengers, carriers, maidservants, and slaves; otherwise, they are combatants, carry weapons, and make war like real adults. Often, the type of recruitments is different for boys and girls: the boys are useful for combats in the front line and in other military activities, whereas the girls are more frequently used as sexual slaves and forced laborers. Also, children who live in zones of conflict or in its vicinity, the same as separated and nonaccompanied children, are even more exposed to the risk of military recruitment, whether it is done by official and nonofficial members of governments.[19]

1.2.1   The recruitment by force

Contrary to armed forces in Western countries, where joining an army is voluntary, some of the armed forces (rebellious or revolutionary armies, the guerrilla, paramilitary, or other forces) in other parts of the world recruit young people by force or under the threat to be killed, and they are obliged to carry weapons. In the north of Uganda, for example, young people from seven to fifteen years old are kidnapped and forced by Joseph Kony—the chief of "the Lord's Army"—to fight in his army. To escape this forced recruitment, children who are known as the *night commuters* leave every day their houses before sunset to take refuge in a camp "in order to stay alive and to see a new day."[20] Other examples of recruitments by force can

---

[19]   UNITED NATIONS HIGH COMMISSIONER FOR REFUGEES, Sexual and Gender-Based Violence Against Refugees, Returnees, and Internally Displaced Persons: Guidelines for Prevention and Response, New York, United Nations, 2003, p. 79.

[20]   Keith MORRISSON, "Children of War in Northern Uganda," Dateline

be seen in a decision of the high commissioner of the United Nations for the Refugees in favor of an ex-child soldier: "the applicant was forced, during his childhood, to serve in the Angolan army as a child soldier. He was subject to three recruitments, one after the other, in a training camp of the MPLA. He underwent very hard trainings and has witnessed several executions of young children who complained."[21]

1.2.2   The voluntary recruitment

Voluntarism is an alternate or complementary form of recruitment to the obligatory military service. The terms of this contractual recruitment are regulated by the countries' own rules of law. However, regarding child soldiers, there are cases where the child decides, of his sound judgment, to join a rebel group or government force to fight or take justice in his own hands. The child, in this case, wants either to avenge the death of a member of his family or wants to contribute actively to a cause.[22] For example, in ex-Yugoslavia, young teenagers between the ages of ten and seventeen years—members of the two extreme groups in the armed conflict—agreed to be integrated in irregular or paramilitary forces thinking that it is their duty, as a patriot, to fight the enemy.[23]

In Rwanda, most of the Hutu youth decided to join the voluntary militia and was trained with sticks and machetes, which is a way to prepare themselves for the genocide of the minority group of Tutsis. In fact, according to Alison Desforges, historian of Human Rights Watch, "the interahamwe had hidden many weapons; they had trained

---

NBC, 22 August 2005.

[21] SPF/N° 452653, 28 May 2004.

[22] Rachel HARVEY, *Children and armed conflict: a guide to international humanitarian and human rights law*, Essex, University of Essex, 2003, p. 26.

[23] Gaetan LAVOIE, "Right to Speak: Can the Children of War find Peace?" Télé-Québec, 2001.

1,700 young people in various districts of Kigali; their chief said that they could kill 1,000 Tutsis in 20 minutes."[24] Enlisted in irregular forces, called vigilante brigades, these child soldiers were regarded as "young policemen who were charged to take care of the safety of their family and their neighbourhoods."[25] These types of recruitment, whether they are legal or illegal, always have causes and effects: the warlord, with his political ambitions, takes the child with him in a structural violence that we see in those armed conflicts where one can believe that physical, social, and psychological traumatisms will follow. These psychological and emotional war syndromes will generate, for sure, resentments, fears, and hatreds that will feed the conflicts of tomorrow.[26]

1.3 The causes for children recruitment

The armed conflict in Sierra Leone, which is regarded by many as "a foolish war," cost many lives and limbs to hundreds of thousands of people, of which several are considered victims at the hands of child soldiers. In fact, five thousand to ten thousand children were recruited by rebel forces and the army. It is necessary to understand that in similar situations, those people who recruit these children do it with impunity particularly when there is a quasi absence of monitoring during conflicts. If the children are recruited by paramilitary groups or armed forces, it is because the warlords largely require their assistance, and those children themselves are often unable to say no.

---

[24] Danièle LACOURSE, "Rwanda: Chronicle of an Announced Genocide," Alter-Ciné, Inc., 1996.

[25] HUMAN RIGHTS COMMISSION, Marie-Thérèse Bocoum: Response from the parties concerned and dialogue with the delegations, New York, United Nations, 6 November 2002.

[26] A/51/306/Add.1, 6 September 1996.

1.3.1 From the interest of recruiters or warlords

The contribution of child soldiers to these armed groups is important under their recruiters' human resources plan. Although children are recruited because they are obedient, very motivated, devoted, and easy to handle, these children—once recruited and engaged in violent wars—will be regarded as collateral damage by the warlords. The official reasons that several of these armed conflicts exist are based on social claims coming from one or several groups. However, the real causes of these conflicts are closely related to political and economic objectives: the need to be powerful while having the power of life and death on a given group and the need to control the public treasury for personal gains. In fact, the Sierra Leone war has started in 1990 by the rebels to control the diamond fields. It was the same situation with the warlord Charles Taylor of Liberia,[27] where thousands of young people were recruited to protect the government's assets: gold mines and diamond layers. By doing this, the boy child soldiers repress, kidnap, rape, kill, and keep the streets in a climate of fear and terror, while the young girls, if they are not killed or do not kill for them, are used to attract future child soldiers or forced to have sexual intercourse with their superiors.[28]

1.3.2 From the vulnerability of recruits or future child soldiers

If children are left to enlist in paramilitary groups and then become involved in armed conflicts, it is because many of them are incapable—except for forced recruitment—to solve pressing economic problems: poverty prevents them from meeting their basic

---

[27] Robert CORNELLIER, Patricio HENRIQUEZ, and Raymonde PROVENCHER, "Assassinated Childhood," Macumba International, Extremis Series, Télé-Québec, 2001.

[28] China KEITESI, *The Little Girl with the Kalashnikov: My Life as a Child Soldier*, Brussels, Éditions GRIP, 2004, p. 264.

needs (often armed groups give them food, clothes, and money). There are children who are enlisted in armed groups because of their patriotism or their desire to fulfill a childhood dream through the violence they have seen in the media. Other children are enrolled to protect themselves or their families who are threatened by members of radical groups. Because of their innocence, their small body, their intellectual limit, or their "immaturity," these kids let themselves to be manipulated by propaganda that dictates their actions. This aspect of youth "brainwashing" usually appears in various conflicts around the world. Indeed, before the genocide in Rwanda, the radio stations were already playing pro-government propaganda card to mobilize young Hutu. For example, Radio Television Libre des Mille Collines (RTLM), in particular, encourages the Hutu majority group to violence against the minority Tutsi, "The Inkotanyi (the Tutsis) are of unparalleled ferocity. These are among the hyenas of hyenas, more wicked than the rhino (...) the Tutsi cockroaches have a thirst for blood (...) we must fight the Tutsi inkotanyi, exterminate them, and sweep them across this country because there is no refuge for them! We will exterminate them much easier for it is only one ethnic group. Look at the size of a person, see her pretty little nose and then break it! We need to get some sticks, cudgels, machetes and reload to prevent damage to our country!"[29] With this kind of discourse from the RTLM, Simon Dring[30] understands very well the problem of propaganda facing by a child soldier. In his remarks on the psychological state of the child during war, he said that a young soldier who commits a crime for obeying orders, or because he is forced by

---

[29] *Supra*, note 24.

[30] Managing director of EKNSHEY Television and former reporter for the *Daily Telegraph*; the only foreign journalist who covered the Bangladesh War of Independence between Pakistan in 1971. *Infra*, bibliography, Raymonde PROVENCHER, "War Babies," Macumba International, Télé-Québec, 2002.

circumstances or by his own fear, experiences terrifying emotions; ultimately, "only education prevents us from committing such crimes."

1.4 The effects of children recruitment

There cannot be causes without effects when the enlistment of children into armed forces or armed groups is based on social, political, and economic factors of such countries. Once recruited, these children are exposed to the worst dangers and experience the worst suffering, both psychological and physical. According to the report of Graça Machel, which led to the creation of the first mandate for children affected by war, child soldiers who are abducted, detained in military camps, and forced to kill have lived and suffered traumatic experiences.[31]

1.4.1 The immediate effects

The immediate effects on physical and mental condition of children have a direct link to their recruitment into armed conflict. These consequences are also very visible. These children may suffer from anxiety because they are separated from their families. These children may have nightmares or become insomniacs, and they can stop playing and laughing, lose appetite, and avoid all contact. The worst effect is when the child was forced to kill other children as soldiers who tried to desert. This was the case of an Angolan child who, after two suicide attempts, was accused of treason and had to suffer mistreatment and torture.[32]

---

[31] *Supra,* note 26.

[32] *Supra,* note 21.

1.4.2   The long-term effects

The recruitment of children and the effects of war on these children will leave serious physical and psychological consequences that will manifest itself as violence. These children may have trouble concentrating in class. Older children and adolescents may become anxious or depressed, losing all hope in the future or having aggressive behavior.[33] In fact, according to Father Chama Caballero, director of Camp St. Michael in Sierra Leone,[34] "On a psychological level, they are all totally demolished" for life. This psychological aspect of armed conflict plays an important influence on other aspects such as legal aspects in relation to the delinquency of the child in society. Also, "the sexual abuse of boys, especially girls, during their military recruitment may have important sociocultural implications that may impact negatively on their (...) social reintegration after their demobilization."[35]

---

[33] *Supra*, note 26.

[34] *Supra*, note 27.

[35] HIGH COMMISSIONER, *op. cit.*, note 19, p. 79.

CHAPTER 2

The Paradoxical Status of Child Soldiers: Victims and Aggressors

For international law, the notion of child soldiers defies the traditional distinction between the category of children and adults.[36] In general, "if we do not recognize in child soldiers' attributes that are associated with childhood (e.g., vulnerability), we do not recognize either those attributes that are necessary to become adult soldiers (the sense of responsibility or the ethics of war)."[37] In this case, international law remains ambiguous regarding the legal status of child soldiers and hesitates between the legal concept of victims and the aggressors. There is indeed a paradox in the definition of child soldier: the child is a victim as well as a perpetrator. Given the ignorance of this international law paradox, the child becomes an easier target for recruitment, and this encourages him to continue his acts of delinquency. Finally, as it was already mentioned on the immediate and long-term effects, this paradox also creates serious consequences for the physical and mental development of children.

2.1 The concept of "child victim"

A victim, according to the dictionary of international law, is a person who has suffered harm because of an internationally wrongful

---

[36] N. ARZOUMANIAN and F. PIZZUTELLI, *loc. cit.*, note 3, p. 827.

[37] Alcinda HONWANA, Innocents and Guilty: Child Soldiers as Tactical Actors, University of Cape Town, The African File/Politics, "Children, Youth and Politics," Cap, 2000, n° 80, p. 59.

act. Also, "victims are people who, individually or collectively, suffered harm including impairment of bodily or mental injury, emotional suffering, economic loss or substantial impairment of their fundamental rights, because of acts or omissions that violate criminal laws that are enforced in a Member State, including those laws proscribing criminal abuse of power."[38] Thus, the term "victims of war" contains general terms, although having no technical meaning in international law means all people that international humanitarian law seeks to protect and who are affected by the effects of armed conflict. The impact of armed conflict on children shows that thousands of girls are victims of rape and other forms of sexual violence and abduction of children has become increasingly systematic and widespread.[39] Also, since 2003, more than fourteen million children are forced to abandon their homes, whether inside or outside their country of origin. Each year, between eight thousand and ten thousand children are killed or maimed by mines.[40] Since the armed conflict in Bosnia,[41] the international community considers urgent to provide assistance to child soldiers, particularly in cases where they are considered victims, especially when they were abducted and forcibly recruited.

2.2 The concept of "child aggressor"

An attacker, according to the dictionary of international law, is the author of an act of aggression. This definition is endorsed by the United Nations International Law Commission that defines an aggressor as "any individual who, as leader or organizer, actively participates in or ordered the planning, preparation, initiation or

---

[38] AG Rés. 40/34, 29 November 1985, § 1.

[39] *Supra*, note 2.

[40] *Id.*

[41] CS Rés. 752, 15 May 1992, § 7.

waging of aggression committed by a state."[42] Certainly, if this attack must be committed by a state, the individual who works for the state as an agent of that state is also liable. However, can a child be an agent of a government and be responsible for a crime against humanity as an aggressor? In some cases, such as Lucien Badjeko, the child may be considered an aggressor. Lucien, as he explains in his book,[43] volunteered in the Congolese army during the reign of Laurent Kabila, who was a rebel and later chairman of the Democratic Republic of Congo (DRC). Lucian, born into a wealthy family, has his dream of becoming a "Rambo" or a "Schwarzenegger" type African soldier. After enlisting voluntarily in the Congolese army, he was promoted *afande*.[44] This new promotion has allowed him to lead the newly recruited children and raping girls. Also, as a commander, he has the power of life and death over some of its soldiers who are older than him. He even ordered the soldiers to attack military bases and other strategic points. If the case of Lucien Badjeko is well documented, there are other cases that are not.

2.3 The consequences of the paradoxical status of child soldier

At national and international law levels, "the association of terms of child and child soldier is a paradox, insofar as these child soldiers are in the interstitial space between these two categories."[45] The paradoxical status of the child soldier brings consequences for the physical and psychological condition of the child when he becomes adult. The child soldier, mentally and physically handicapped, may become a threat to himself and his environment. There are

---

[42] Art. 16 ACDI.

[43] Lucien BADJOKO and Katia CLARENS, *I Was a Child Soldier: The Poignant Story of an African Childhood*, Paris, Éditions Plon, 2005, p. 162.

[44] Means "chief" or "commander" in Swahili language.

[45] A. HONWANA, *op. cit.*, note 37, n° 80, p. 59.

also sociocultural implications that may negatively influence the reunification of families or social reintegration of child soldiers after their demobilization.[46] Without some form of rehabilitation before returning to his environment, the child will probably be dismissed and demonized by his peers.

Marginalized and deprived of social assistance and family support, the child—now lawless—needs only to report to his "base" to become part of a new armed group, which is very often under the control of a government or a corrupt state in directing them to commit illegal acts that are becoming more and more shocking. However, until we decided not to consider the legal and paradoxical status of child soldiers, among victims and perpetrators, armed groups and government forces will continue to use these children and equip them. On the contrary, if we accept the idea that these child soldiers are both victims and aggressors, international justice would be better able to take care of these children, who would be rehabilitated according to international standards. International law—namely, the members of the international community—would have to establish an International Court of Juvenile Justice (ICJJ) with the sole purpose of supporting records on crimes of genocide and crimes against humanity that are committed by these children warriors. In fact, in establishing this court and in holding those children responsible, international law would be able to prevent further recruitment and to provide effective assistance to the rehabilitation of these youth, for the child—knowing that he will be judged by a high court of international justice—would be able, except for forced recruitment, to refuse voluntarily to be enlisted in an armed group.

Indeed, in certain cases, a child has the ability to think, and reason seems to be sometimes higher than in adults. For example, when

---

[46] HIGH COMMISSIONER, *op. cit.*, note 19, p. 79.

natural law says it is immoral to kill and that positive law declares it is unlawful to kill, the child understands well that killing is a bad thing. While the child understands and accepts unequivocally this type of reasoning, the adult—on his part—will try to find a specific reason or a criterion for saying that killing someone, in certain specific circumstances, such as war, self-defense, etc., is justifiable. Thus, the reasoning is straightforward in children while it is complex in adults. In fact, in general, eight-to-twelve-year-old children meet with as much relevance as adults in matters involving their logical reasoning ability.[47] Therefore, some children have a free and an open choice to join or not an armed group. In such cases, a child who commits a "serious crime"[48] should be able to appear before the International Court of Juvenile Justice. This does not mean that the child should be tried as an adult, but the idea of giving justice to victims of acts committed by a child soldier should be a priority.

In fact, paradoxically, the appearance of child soldiers before the International Court of Juvenile Justice would make decisions more focused on the needs of rehabilitating them. We know that certain norms of international law focus on the administration of juvenile justice, primarily to ensure the rights and freedoms of children in the judicial process.[49] These standards fall into a logical ____, however,

---

[47] Jean BARATGIN and Ira NOVECK, "Not only base rates are neglected on the engineer-lawyer problem: An investigation of reasoners under utilization of complementary," (2000), 29 M. and R. 86. *Infra*, appendix (figure 1).

[48] There are seven types of "serious crimes" we can call "deadly sins" that are prosecuted by the American justice if a child commits one of these following: murder, rape, aggravated child molestation, aggravated sodomy, aggravated sexual battery, voluntary manslaughter, and armed robbery with a firearm. And, if one of these crimes is committed by a juvenile or someone who is less than eighteen years of age, he will be prosecuted as an adult. Cf. *Juvenile Justice and Delinquency Prevention Act*, 42 USC § 5601 (2002). See also *State of Georgia*, Senate Bill 440 (SB 440), 1994.

[49] *Minimum Rules for the Administration of Juvenile Justice* (Beijing Rules, 29 November 1985), *Rules for the Protection of Juveniles Deprived of their Liberty* (14

upon the shoulders of the states—and not to international justice, to decide what the relevant guidelines for juvenile delinquency are. However, some countries have extremely repressive reactions when confronted with crimes committed by child soldiers. For example, despite the international ban on use of the death penalty against minors,[50] the Democratic Republic of Congo (DRC) has returned a verdict of death penalty against child soldiers. Youth, such as Babuyu Oleko, Nanasi Kisala, and five other child soldiers were all judged by a military tribunal for the DRC.[51] Oleko died in prison, Kisala was released, and five others had their death sentences commuted to life imprisonment; then, later, they received a presidential pardon that allowed them to stay in prison for five years because of the crimes they have committed.[52] In stating that international law wants to focus only on recruiters, the international community leaves child soldiers to the vagaries of internal justice, which may be insensitive to their injuries and their urgent needs of reeducation.

Still, holding the child accountable for his crimes makes sense only insofar as the sentence he receives is consistent with the principles of rehabilitation and repair that must animate the juvenile justice system, as demonstrated eloquently by relevant standards and international treaties. However, in a state of lawlessness, the legal system is incapable of doing justice to victims, and, more importantly, in the rare cases where the crimes of child soldiers are found, sanctions imposed seem influenced by revenge than any other thing. However, juvenile justice should not be punitive but based on the objectives of rehabilitation

---

December 1990), *Guidelines for the Prevention of Juvenile Delinquency* (Riyadh Guidelines, 14 December 1990), and the *Vienna Guidelines on Children in the Criminal Justice System* (21 July 1997).

[50] ACT 50/007/2002, 25 September 2002.

[51] COD 270401.4.EE, 19 May 2003.

[52] *Id.*

and repair. In fact, juvenile justice has several goals: not only empower young offenders from their victims and their communities for the offenses committed, since citizens must live in a safe community and have security, but also and ultimately reduce crime and victimization of youth through programs of prevention. Young people (victims and perpetrators) that fall under this system should come out from their rehabilitative environment when they are ready to become responsible and productive members in their communities. The refusal of international law to accept the dual status of child soldiers allows some governments to abuse and violate twice the rights and freedoms of these children instead of helping them become responsible citizens. Thus, first, the child [attacker] is used by a warlord to carry out its dirty work; and, second, once the work is done, the child [victim] would be imprisoned or executed under the order of the same warlord who sometimes becomes the head of state.

2.3.1   An opportunity for the systemic recruitment of children

The problem of child soldiers in Africa has enabled these children to become specimens in the study of the impact of armed conflict on children.[53] In fact, "Liberia, Somalia and Rwanda have shown in all its horror Africa's inability to resolve its conflicts and humanitarian tragedies."[54] Indeed, "the persistence of social injustice and the discontinuity of democratic processes have combined to create these tragedies."[55] These tragedies, including the recruitment of children into paramilitary and armed forces, continue to be perpetuated in other parts of the world where one finds the same forms of social

---

[53]   N. ARZOUMANIAN and F. PIZZUTELLI, *loc. cit.*, note 3, p. 827.

[54]   *Statement of the First Regional Consultation on the Impact of Armed Conflict on Children in the Horn of Africa and in East, Central and Southern Africa. Addis Ababa, April 17–19, 1995.*

[55]   *Id.*

injustice that are due in part to poor governance. However, when one speaks of "mismanagement," it also means "incompetence" and "corruption" that often link discredited politicians trying to exploit the population to remain in power.

In these laboratories full of tragedies, the paradoxical status of the child soldier allows the child to be an easier target for recruitment. On the one hand, easy to mishandle with his dream of saving his country or to help his family and to become a leader in his own ranks, the child [attacker] can deliberately violate and kill at will and still be considered as a victim because of armed conflicts or when the power relationship is reversed. On the other hand, in a situation of dependency and under high pressure of a gang leader, the child [victim] openly commits barbaric acts to benefit from the grace and blessings of his boss. In addition, when the child [victim] has no family to support him after his discharge, the child has nothing to lose or win and he could be recruited again while deciding to live a life of crime and debauchery. In accepting the dual status of the child soldier, international law would be able to strengthen its controls by developing real programs of prevention, awareness, and propaganda against recruiting. It is a way to be proactive with respect to the impact of armed conflict on children.

Systemic recruitment of children is a global scourge. The problems that are related to the recruitment, use, and involvement of children in armed conflict are numerous. We cannot ignore that these children who are under the control of warlords in Afghanistan, Indonesia, Colombia, Haiti, and other parts of the world are aggressors as well as victims. In fact, the female Ugandan China Keitetsi, now an adult, says that some of these child soldiers "gave the impression of having already experienced [armed conflicts], others were new and inexperienced" in learning to shelter and attack with the bayonet.[56] In Darfur, Congo-DRC, Palestine, Iraq, and elsewhere, the same situation repeats itself: naïve and innocent children will become true warrior machines and child soldiers.

2.3.1.1   Impunity for recruiters or warlords

The recruitment systemic of *kadogos*[57] was done without fear. The warlords solidify their power through arbitrary arrests, summary executions, and forced disappearances. Armed groups continue to commit rape and other forms of sexual violence. In addition to the mass rapes and mutilations, these warlords are not afraid to commit murder, torture, massacre of civilians and political opponents, loot shops and private houses, burn houses, and raze villages entirely.

For several decades of armed conflict around the world, some warlords have never been questioned in relation to the systemic recruitment of children. In fact, Thomas Lubanga Dyilo—leader of the Congolese Patriots Union (CPU)—has become "the only warlord indicted after being accused of enlisting and conscripting child soldiers and their use and active participation in armed conflict in Ituri,"[58] a province of the Democratic Republic of Congo (DRC). However, one wonders why the international community has now decided to grab the collar of Thomas Lubanga. Of all the warlords who live in Kinshasa, Kampala, and Kigali, why Lubanga? There may be two hypotheses we can analyze to understand the move and the actions of the international authorities to arrest Lubanga. One hypothesis is taken from a declaration of Lubanga's lawyer, Jean Flamme, a Belgian. He

---

[56]   C. KEITESI, *op. cit.*, note 28, p. 90.

[57]   "Child soldiers" or "little things with no value" (Swahili language).

[58]   Didier SAMSON, "International Justice: A Congolese warlord before the ICC," Radio France Internationale, 20 March 2006.

stated, "There are pursuing people who have no political or financial resources; but, those with national and international sponsors remain unscathed."[59] Does this statement that was made by Mr. Flamme mean that very powerful countries and members of the international community prefer to ignore the systemic recruitment of children because of their personal interests in the region? The second hypothesis is based on the murder of nine Bangladeshi peacekeepers, members of the United Nations peacekeeping mission in Congo-DRC, in February 2005. Following the killings, international organizations were convinced of the direct involvement of Thomas Lubanga in the violence in Ituri and had begun to prepare a record that is classified as "serious crimes."[60]

Considering this legal case preparedness, we wonder on the rapidity of the international community: should the international community wait for his own people, the peacekeepers or the "blue helmets," to be killed before they act so as not to repeat past mistakes, especially as they failed to act during the Rwandan genocide? If yes, how can we assess the lives of thousands of Africans compared to the lives of nine peacekeepers? One may wonder whether the arrest of Lubanga is in good faith and sincere, if it is really aimed at ending the recruitment and conscription of child soldiers.

In fact, if the arrest of Lubanga is in good faith and is made to allow the international community to end the recruitment and conscription of children in armed conflict, the arrest must be justified and be appreciated. Indeed, Thomas Lubanga—arrested in Kinshasa and imprisoned in the Netherlands—is not a saint. In fact, in Congo-DRC, he was called the butcher of Ituri; and his thousands of child

---

[59] Stéphanie MAUPAS, "A Former Congolese Warlord Prosecuted for Recruiting Child Soldiers," Radio France Internationale, 9 November 2006.

[60] *Supra*, note 58.

soldiers, known to everyone and everywhere as "the erasers,"[61] practiced a policy of systematic elimination of men, women, and children. With respect to the physical and systematic elimination of civilians, on August 31, 2002, the Congolese Patriots Union (CPU) has massacred the members of the village of Songolo where over 140 women and children were killed in their sleep. In November 2002, another massacre has happened in the town of Mongbwalu, where over 200 people were killed. Later, on December 6, 2002, another massacre took place this time in the city of Kilo, where men, women, and children were forced to dig their own graves.[62] It is estimated that this practice has caused the deaths of more than sixty thousand civilians and displaced over six hundred thousand people out of their territory.[63] The case of African children exemplifies the impunity that exists against the systemic recruitment of these children are mostly supported once the armed conflict ended. Again, there is another problem. The various programs of the United Nations (UN), such as the program of Disarmament, Demobilization, and Reintegration (DDR), have not been effective. Often assisted by volunteer and nonprofit organizations, governments are making a mockery official disarmament ceremony, which leaders have no interest to demobilize and rehabilitate these children warriors.[64]

And, what can we say about those surveillance programs against the enlistment and conscription of children into armed groups? Very disappointing. The reality is different, especially when international

---

[61] This term comes from the English verb "to erase," which means to remove or eliminate, and it was also taken from the title of the Arnold Schwarzenegger's movie *Eraser*.

[62] HUMAN RIGHTS WATCH, *Crimes committed by the UPC in Ituri: 2002–2003*, Brussels, Human Rights Watch, 2006, p. 2.

[63] S/2004/573, 16 July 2004.

[64] L. BADJOKO and K. CLARENS, *op. cit.*, note 43, p. 162.

law is supposed to protect children. In fact, it is understood that "the difficulty of monitoring and documenting the most serious violations and enforcement of international standards in the field has hindered the efforts of several key players; current monitoring and documentation capabilities of the United Nations are limited by ad hoc interventions and poor coordination within its own system."[65]

2.3.1.2   Standardization of children recruitment

According to some, the ambiguity of the concept of child soldier explains the "terrible dilemma"[66] posed by the issue of responsibility for these children in the event of their eventual indictment for crimes under international law.[67] In fact, the International Criminal Court (ICC) has no jurisdiction over a person who was under eighteen at the time of the commission of a crime.[68] The jurisdiction of the court not to prosecute children under eighteen years results in a kind of standardization in their recruitment. The child aggressor and the child victim, facing the impunity given to warlords, are forced to join armed groups regardless of the different impacts this may have on and around them. While the child [aggressor] may see some of the advantages of joining an armed group, the child [victim]—with the exception of those children who are getting used very quickly of being a child soldier—can never comply with this new life, but they obey any order just to survive.[69] Although the child [aggressor] has often the choice of not being recruited; the child [victim], on the other hand, is forced to be a killer. The warlord, on the other side, welcomes the confusion

---

[65]   Olara OTUNNU, "Protecting Children in War: How to Set Up an Effective Monitoring and Documentation System," (2004) 41 Chro. des N.U. 69.

[66]   S/2000/915, 4 October 2000, § 33.

[67]   N. ARZOUMANIAN and F. PIZZUTELLI, loc. cit., note 3, p. 827.

[68]   Art. 26 SR-CPI.

[69]   C. KEITESI, op. cit., note 28, p. 90.

that international law provides to the legal status of a child soldier, while the same law does not either make him responsible for the recruitment of these children, for when the law is not set in motion to address the violation of international laws, the violators have nothing to fear.

This feeling of being above the law, given the dual legal status of the child soldier, makes it easier for recruiters or warlords to systemically standardize the recruitment of children. Childhood, already regarded as a "transitional phenomenon,"[70] is projected faster in the adult world. When he actually reaches his majority, the child is integrated into the regular armed forces and become a full-fledged soldier with his many war experiences like a veteran.

The rapid advance in the recruitment of children is seen everywhere. For example, in 1996 in Zaire, which is now Congo-DRC, Laurent Kabila has politicized Congolese children with patriotic speeches in places frequented by young people.[71] This allowed him to be at the head of the Alliance of Democratic Forces for the Liberation of Congo (ADFLC), a group of armed rebels consisting particularly of ten thousand child soldiers aged between seven and sixteen years.[72] In November 2002, in the Democratic Republic of Congo (DRC), Thomas Lubanga entered a primary school and has gathered by force about forty elementary schoolchildren from the sixth-grade level to join his army, the Congolese Patriots Union (CPU). The same "recruitment operation" was done also at Solongo.[73] In the Middle

---

[70] R. HARVEY, *op. cit.*, note 22, p. 26.

[71] Often addressed to young people by "The Call of the Flag."

[72] INTERNATIONAL LABOUR ORGANIZATION, *Wounded childhood: Taking stock of ten years of civil war in Central Africa*, Geneva, ILO/IPEC, 2003, p. 5.

[73] HUMAN RIGHTS WATCH, *op. cit.*, note 62, p. 3.

East, especially in Palestine, youth suicide bombers, called "martyrs," are exploding themselves in the streets of the state of Israel to end its occupation of Palestinian territories. In Colombia, guerrillas used child soldiers in a war without end to fight against the Colombian government. In Haiti, in 1994, young "lavalas" or "chimeres" are armed to root out the opposition camp to consolidate the power for their leader, Jean-Bertrand Aristide, who was also the president of Haiti. Finally, in Iraq, Afghanistan, and Pakistan, armed groups of extremists and terrorists working for Al-Qaeda and the Taliban are recruiting children as suicide bombers against those they are considering "infidels," people who do not share their religious beliefs. Most of the time, they ended up killing their own countrymen, women, and children.

2.3.1.3   Utilization and implication of children in armed conflicts

The use and involvement of children in armed conflict cannot be achieved without the benediction of international law, which has given this extraordinary impunity to warlords. Impunity has also resulted in the standardization of recruitment of children, already having a dual legal status, who are not criminally liable. The decision of the International Criminal Court (ICC), which refuses to consider the cases of "serious crimes" committed by child soldiers who are under eighteen years of age, has affected the lives and environment of these children. On the one hand, the child soldier—who can be both aggressor and victim—is mentally and emotionally affected for the rest of his life. On the other hand, the barbaric acts that are committed by child soldiers are becoming more intense with incredible violence.

By refusing to consider these issues, international law accepts that any act committed by a child soldier be treated and cared for under the provisions of internal law. However, very often (when it comes to Africa, where the recruitment and conscription of children are done systemically), the judicial apparatus of the country that will have the record of the child is in direct conflict with international standards. How can a government, in ratifying certain international and regional instruments, be subject to international law when the same government violated deliberately or through ignorance the rights that they are called to protect? Worse, the authorities who oversee the judiciary process, to administer justice for minors, have themselves sometimes recruited children.[74] In this case, how can we accept that a child soldier who is accused of genocide or crimes against humanity be tried by such a judicial system? One reason: international law does not want to be held responsible and prefers to ignore the dual status of the child soldier. It was estimated that over two million child soldiers have died in war for the last ten years, while between four million and five million are injured or remain disabled. In addition, approximately one million child soldiers were orphaned during the time of their recruitment, while three hundred thousand are currently involved in armed conflicts around the world.[75]

Indeed, according to the Canadian Romeo Dallaire, former colonel of UN forces in Rwanda during the genocide, children are used as a weapon of war by an opponent against another, especially as shields.[76] In fact, we cannot ignore it.[77] But, if we understand that these children are used by some as shields, others use them as genuine war machines. These are machines that can be controlled to act without

---

[74] *Supra*, note 51, particularly about *the Babuyu Oleko and Nanasi Kisala case against the Military Court Order of the Democratic Republic of Congo (DRC)*. *Infra*, appendix (figure 4, jurisprudence) E/CN.4/2002/74/Add.2, 8 May 2002, § 240.

[75] *Supra*, note 23.

[76] *Id.*

[77] C. KEITESI, *op. cit.*, note 28, p. 92.

mercy—machines that torture, kill, and destroy. Admittedly, many called those child soldiers "despoilers of vaginas" and "little things of nothing" who use rape as a weapon of war as well as a weapon of mass destruction.[78]

The use and involvement of children in armed conflict in the Democratic Republic of Congo (DRC) has a great impact on several generations of children who voluntarily participated in armed conflict. Between 1996 and 1997, with the aim of overthrowing the dictator Mobutu, Laurent Desire Kabila had recruited thousands of children to counteract the advancing of pro-government troops.[79] Kabila had a blind belief in the deadly force and the submission of these child soldiers to seize power. He considered these child soldiers like his own children, and he himself called them "his children" who would do him no harm.[80] Once in Kinshasa, Kabila declared himself president under the strong protection of his army of children. However, a few years later, those child soldiers of Kabila had become adults, and they had developed their own political ambitions after realizing they had been used and manipulated. Suspecting a revolt among these emancipated child soldiers, Kabila gave them a bitter lesson: forty-seven *kadogos* were arrested and executed for treason.[81] The next day, on January 16, 2001, a child soldier named Rashidi Kasereka, who was a member of the close security of Kabila, came into the palace and executed the warlord.[82]

---

[78] BOLYA, *Desecration of the Vaginas: Rape as a Weapon of War and Weapon of Mass Destruction*, Paris, Éditions Le Serpent à Plumes, 2002, p. 85.

[79] UNICEF, *Situation "Child soldiers,"* Paris, Unicef France, 2004, p. 1-66.

[80] Out of respect, child soldiers call Kabila "the Wise" or "the old man" (Mzé) in the Swahili language.

[81] Charles ONNYANGO-OBBO, "Why nobody's dancing on Kabila's grave," The East African, 19–21 February 2001.

[82] Stephen SMITH, "These Child Soldiers Who Killed Kabila," Le Monde, 10 February 2001.

2.3.2   The systematic delinquency of children

Crime and juvenile delinquency are rising because of psychological effects that mimic the violence among children who are affected by armed conflict.[83] Being armed with a Kalashnikov gives the child the power to be violent and aggressive.[84] In fact, once the child is recruited and becomes a soldier, he has the power of life and death on civilians and prisoners of "war" as well as the people he kidnapped and raped. The child soldier, who seems daunting and tough, is young and does not seem to have pity. Sometimes, he is the sole judge and may decide today, at this time and at any moment, which places or people should he be imposed on the next penalty. Aside from acts of war crimes and genocide he committed during armed conflict, even after his discharge from the armed conflict, the child can be dangerous, though he is himself a victim. He forgets his dual legal status especially that of being considered an aggressor because of its virtual immunity from being a child soldier. He is now a child with many field experiences who would be easy to recruit again as a soldier who would not contradict his superiors—a soldier who would have more desire to learn the art of war and to kill again without remorse. For the child, whether international law grants immunity to his recruiter, he is asking himself why the same immunity would not be given to him. Why should he be held liable? Who is he unless he is another child soldier whom international law will continue to ignore?

International law defines a juvenile as "a child or young person who is accused or convicted of committing a crime," which means any conduct (act or omission) that is punishable by law under the legal system.[85] With the result of his recruitment into the army and his

---

[83]   CRC/C/SR.548, 3 November 1999.

[84]   *Supra*, note 30.

[85]   Article 2.2, the *Beijing Rules. Cf.* AG Res. 40/33, 29 November 1985.

involvement in conflicts, the child was exposed to a structural violence that has impacted him physically, socially, and psychologically. The child, struggling with emotional and psychological trauma that causes resentment, fears, and hatreds, which will fuel his actions,[86] began to wander the streets in begging and engaging in delinquency.[87] The veteran child soldier, becoming disabled, also suffers from mental and physical disabilities. The young combatant, in difficult circumstances, is now in conflict with the law. He becomes a street child, a drug addict, or a refugee.[88] His legal status, though paradoxical, has never changed, and the child [victim or perpetrator] will reproduce the same violence, which he knows well. For the boys, the tendency to use violence when necessary will be systematic. He begins to lead a life of crime by first refusing to obey the rules of adults or authorities; and then he will start using or continue to use drugs, under typical exclusion from the society, in undertaking other forms of violence.[89] However, it may be that addiction is not sufficient or necessary for the child soldier, but instead he chooses to be employed in drug trafficking and illegal selling of firearms.[90] However, for the girls who were recruited for sexual exploitation, physical and psychological trauma are more severe: injury or loss of virginity, psychological problems that lead to the loss of dignity, early pregnancy, sexually transmitted diseases, such as HIV/AIDS, prostitution, and violence toward others.[91]

---

[86] *Supra*, note 26.

[87] *Declaration of the Burundian Human Rights League ITEKA on the International Day of the African Child*, 16 June 2002.

[88] *Supra*, note 83.

[89] *Summary of the Work and Recommendations of the Child Delegates: Regional Consultation on Violence Against Children in West and Central Africa*, Bamako, Mali, May 24-25, 2005.

[90] SOWC/04/F/06, 14 September 2004.

[91] *Supra*, note 89.

2.3.2.1 Implication of children in acts of delinquency

The main cause of juvenile delinquency [in our society] is a logical consequence of recruitment of children in the [Congolese] public force to deal with civil wars.[92] Once these children begin to wander the streets, girls, for example, are forced into prostitution and are thus more exposed to sexually transmitted diseases.[93] Indeed, in Nicaragua and El Salvador, the legacy of armed conflicts still exists. These children have experienced extreme violence and have been exposed to death, recruitment into armed forces and insurgent groups, the killing of the members of their family, and exile.[94] The notorious crimes committed by children involved in armed conflict in El Salvador still continue to be inventoried in their country of origin as in their host countries even though these children are now adults. While the Observer Mission of the United Nations in El Salvador (ONUSAL) had managed to end violations of human rights that have been motivated by politics, a new threat arose from the ashes of war, urban violence, which generates fear and insecurity in the country. Today, crime is cited as the primary concern of most Salvadorans.[95]

In fact, according to a report by the Institute of Public Opinion at the University of Central America in San Salvador, "the biggest factor contributing to this situation is the rise of groups who were born in these urban areas after the end of the civil war."[96] If during the war in El Salvador, an estimated 80 percent of government

---

[92] Faustin B. LOKASOLA, "Profile and Possible Solutions to the Problem of Juvenile Delinquency in the DRC," Société Civile, 11 July 2004.

[93] *Supra*, note 87.

[94] *Supra*, note 26.

[95] Nicole HERTVIK, "El Salvador: Change from Within," (2002) 39 Chro. des N.U. 85.

[96] *Id.*

forces and 20 percent of recruits from the Farabundo Marti National Liberation Front (FMNL) were aged under eighteen, many of these former child soldiers have left their country of origin to immigrate legally or illegally to other countries. The United States of America is the country where many of these immigrants were welcomed, and former child combatants are grouped under the name of MS-13 in neighborhoods with high concentrations of Mexicans to counter discrimination and abuse from local gangs.[97] This group of immigrants, who initially fought for their rights and freedoms, is now the most dangerous group of criminals (the Third World Momentum) established in over thirty-three states.[98]

With experience gained in military and paramilitary forces, and guerrillas, these former child soldiers who have regularly seen violence will act to defend themselves in an instinctive way through violence. Indeed, they are mostly charged with burglary, drug dealing, smuggling of firearms, extortion, car theft, prostitution, kidnapping, assault with deadly weapons, drive-by shootings, murder, and rape. In fact, in February 2005, one of the former child soldiers, Ebert Anibal Rivera, was arrested by police in Texas.[99] Besides his other paramilitary exploits in Honduras, Rivera was the leader of the notorious Mara Salvatrucha guerrillas, who had fired their weapons at a bus in which twenty-eight passengers were killed.

---

[97] Jim LEHER, "FBI targets MS-13 streets gang," PBS NewsHour Extra, 5 October 2005.

[98] Arian CAMPO-FLORES, "The most dangerous gang in America," *Newsweek,* 28 March 2006.

[99] Frosty WOOLDRIDGE, "MS-13 gangs: immigration's third world momentum," NewsWithViews.com, 14 April 2005.

2.3.2.2   Impunity for child soldiers

The recruitment of children into armed groups is "an excuse or an abuse of power brokers that entrust the work to a child by an adult."[100] However, while the child is often used as a tool of terror, we must admit that the violence used by these children during and after conflicts are inexplicable. These children take part in everything. For many of them, according to China Keitesi, "killing and torturing was an exciting task and a way to satisfy their superiors. The children knew how to use the utmost brutality against prisoners of war for the sole purpose of being promoted to a higher rank."[101] These children perpetuate their acts of "delinquency" and know they will not be held responsible for these acts because of their victim status.

Under international law, criminal liability is a "deterrent" that is often used by a mean of repression, as "the best way to deter criminals and protect the innocent."[102] If so, why does international law not taking charge of the case of these child soldiers who have a very good capacity for discernment and understanding on the battlefield while blindly going forward in the killing of innocents? And why does international law seek to make these children testify in cases of atrocities but help them overcome their psychological traumas that are linked to violence?

International law regards a child soldier [aggressor] as a minor, which is to say "a child or young person who, under the legal system, may have to answer for a crime in a manner different from those

---

[100] INTERNATIONAL COMMITTEE OF THE RED CROSS, *Children in War: Working Document for Delegates to the Armed and Security Forces Concerning the Protection of Children in Situations of Armed Conflict and Unrest*, Geneva, CIRC, 2004, p. 47–60.

[101] C. KEITESI, *op. cit.*, note 28, p. 101.

[102] *Supra*, note 26.

applied in the case of an adult."[103] International law also recognizes that "the threshold of criminal responsibility varies from one country to another"[104] and that "the prosecution must inspire fear of the police."[105] In a context where the age of criminal responsibility is random, should international law not have the rights to make child soldiers accountable for their actions?[106] The international standards for the administration of juvenile justice and other international instruments will not be respected, as international law does not recognize the ambiguity that exists in the legal status of the child soldier. This ignorance of international law opens the door to impunity against child molesters just as it is given to warlords. Impunity, or the lack of punishment after the commission of an act deemed illegal by law, is manifested when the child soldiers can act without harm to themselves or when they are exposed to no risks or to no legal problems.

It is very difficult for us to ignore the paradox that exists in the definition of child soldier as both a victim and an aggressor. Certainly, the impact of armed conflict on children has caused physical, social, and psychological traumas as well as emotional and psychological scars that lead to a reproduction of violence in these children who

---

[103] *Supra*, note 85.

[104] INTERNATIONAL COMMITTEE OF THE RED CROSS, *op. cit.*, note 100, p. 50.

[105] *Supra*, note 26.

[106] N. ARZOUMANIAN and F. PIZZUTELLI, *loc. cit.*, note 3, p. 844. Cf. *Convention on the Rights of the Child*, article 40(3)(a). See also: United Nations Rules for the Protection of Juveniles Deprived of their Liberty, General Assembly Resolution 45/113, UN Doc. A/RES/45/113, December 14, 1990, paragraph 11(a). While international law does not indicate the minimum age of criminal responsibility, the Committee on the Rights of the Child has often noted that the age defined in state law is too low, see Implementation Handbook for *the Convention on the Rights of the Child*, UNICEF, New York, 1998, pp. 551–552. Further, see also the "Beijing Rules," rule 4.

are victims and perpetrators. When we ignore this paradox, we give up—on the one hand—systemic recruitment of children into armed groups. In fact, despite the recruitment of these children, international law places a limitless impunity on both recruiters and warlords. This leads to the normalization of child recruitment, as well as the use and the unconditional involvement of child soldiers in armed conflicts. On the other hand, the routine childhood delinquency [aggressors] turns, during and after conflicts, toward banditry in exploiting deeply the experience they have gained during the war.

Like their aggressors enjoy impunity, these child soldiers also benefit from such impunity as minors (who cannot be held accountable for their actions because of their age) and victims of war (despite a voluntary enlistment and acts committed as "serious crimes"). However, despite the paradox found in the definition of child soldier, international law remains ambiguous in the face of this legal status. Indeed, despite the seriousness of these acts committed by child soldiers, international law believes that there can be no International Juvenile Justice Court and that these children are not responsible for their own actions. In fact, it is understood that "when these are young children who are accused of war crimes, it is obviously necessary to consider re-educate them and not judge them or punish them."[107] In contrast, if these children should be held accountable, they must be supported by domestic law under the national legislation on the criminal responsibility of children to "avoid the risk of conflict between the Statute [of the International Criminal Court] and national legislation about the minimum age of criminal responsibility."[108]

---

[107] *Supra*, note 26.

[108] *Supra*, note 3. *Cf.* Roger S. CLARK and Otto TRIFFTERER, "Article 26: Exclusion of Jurisdiction over Persons under Eighteen," p. 496–497.

In fact, if the internal law of the Democratic Republic of Congo (DRC) was effective enough to arrest, judge, and condemn to death child soldiers such as Babuyu Oleko and Nanasi Kisala, why has this same legal tool not been used to arrest and judge the warlord Thomas Lubanga, accused of enlisting and systemic practice the riding of child soldiers, and thus do justice to its thousands of victims? In fact, in March 2006, United Nations soldiers decided to arrest Thomas Lubanga. Well, if, on the one hand, the instruments of international law do not permit the death sentence for the warlord at the International Criminal Court, why can national law be used blindly against child soldiers despite DRC's ratification of the International Convention on the Rights of the Child (CRC)?

Given the unease of international law to consider these children as aggressors, it is imperative to know how the mechanisms of international humanitarian law and international law of human rights consider the problem of delinquency of child soldiers, particularly when these children are both victims and aggressors.

PART II

The Indecisiveness of International Law regarding the Legal Status of Child Soldiers

CHAPTER 3

The Role of International Law in the Protection of the Rights of the Child

International humanitarian law and international law of human rights play a major role in protecting children's rights especially when dealing with children who are involved in armed conflicts worldwide. In fact, international humanitarian law lays down obligations for the belligerents and the rights to protect persons who are victims of violence in armed conflicts,[109] while the international law of human rights relates to the legal recognition of human dignity and equality between men, women, and children.[110] Instruments concerning human rights specifically set out the expected standards, and humanitarian law must strive to contain their excesses.[111]

3.1 The child and the rules of international humanitarian law

International humanitarian law seeks to regulate the methods of war and treatment of those participating or not participating in war, the behavior of combatants, prisoners of war, wounded soldiers, and civilians.[112] It also rules on the obligations of these fighters and

---

[109] Françoise BOUCHET-SAULNIER, *Practical Dictionary of Humanitarian Law*, Paris, La Découverte & Syros, 2000, p. 163.

[110] *Id.*, p. 156.

[111] *Supra*, note 26.

[112] F. BOUCHET-SAULNIER, *op. cit.*, note 109, p. 56. Cf. Article 43 Protocol I CG defines the word "combatant" as any member of the armed forces of a party to the conflict, except for medical and religious personnel. It is also a term that is mainly used in international conflicts. However, in internal

what they should or should not do. International humanitarian law is the core of human rights and is applied during and after conflicts. These combatants must not only respect the rights and freedoms of every individual, but they must not derogate from certain rights such as rights to liberty and to life, and rights against torture, cruel, and inhuman or degrading treatment. Given that child soldiers are often used in noninternational armed conflicts and can be either commanders or armed individuals who are part of a force or armed group, they are obliged to meet these standards. These noninternational conflicts, often called "civil wars," are conflicts that take place on the territory of a state between the regular armed forces and dissident armed forces or organized armed groups.

3.1.1   Age limit for the conscription of the child soldier

In times of conflicts, international humanitarian law guarantees the child a general protection as a civilian who is not involved in hostilities and, also, a special protection because of his particular vulnerability and helplessness. Indeed, the Rome Statute of the International Criminal Court (ICC) and customary international law argue that the fact of conscripting or enlisting children under the age of fifteen years into armed forces or using them to participate actively in hostilities "constitutes a war crime, whether it is an international or internal armed conflict. The International Criminal Court (ICC) may under certain conditions judge the perpetrators of these crimes, after the entry into force of its statute."[113] The Guiding Principles on

---

conflicts, humanitarian law does not use the term "combatant," since it is difficult to determine or define who is or is not participating in hostilities. A distinction is made between persons who take part in hostilities and those who do not, granting them, depending on the circumstances, the benefit of the protection of the status of prisoner of war or of civilian. *Infra*, appendix (figure 2).

[113] Articles 8.2 (b) (26) and 8.2 (e) (7) SR-CPI.

Internal Displacement within their Own Country, known as Principle 13 or the Guiding Principles of the United Nations, declared that "under no circumstances shall displaced children be recruited into an armed force and required or permitted to participate in fighting. People who are displaced within their own country will be protected against discriminatory practices that leverage their position to enlist in armed forces or armed groups. In particular, any cruel, inhuman or degrading practices that compel a displaced person to accept being conscripted into the army or punish for refusal is prohibited in all circumstances."[114] It is also prohibited to recruit fifteen-to-eighteen-year-old children. Furthermore, these children cannot work when they are under fifteen years of age.[115] In regard to noninternational armed conflicts, Protocol II became the first international document that outlines the problem of noninternational conflicts and describes the fundamental guarantees to the effect that children under fifteen years shall not be recruited in the armed forces or groups or allowed to take part in hostilities.[116] It also important to point at Resolution 1261, which was adopted by the Security Council in 1999 that condemned the recruitment and use of children in armed conflict.[117] However, with the adoption of Resolution 1314 in 2000, for the first time, the international community takes a real stand against the recruitment and involvement or the use of children in armed conflict. In fact, the recruitment of children is seen as "systematic, flagrant and widespread violations of international humanitarian law and the law relating to human rights, including rights of the child," and "these violations may constitute a threat against international peace and security."[118]

---

[114] Annex 2, chapter 10.

[115] Article 77 Protocol I CG.

[116] Art. 4.3 (c) Protocol II CG.

[117] CS Res. 1261, 25 August 1999.

[118] CS Res. 1314, 11 August 2000, § 9.

3.1.2   Serious offenses: between reconciliation and legal prosecutions

Resolution 1379 affirms that armed conflicts usually have many links, such as "terrorism, the illicit trade in precious minerals, the illicit trafficking in small arms and light weapons, and other criminal activities, which can prolong armed conflict or intensify its impact on civilian populations, including children."[119] The same resolution states those governments that are UN members should "put an end to impunity, prosecute those responsible for genocide, crimes against humanity, war crimes and other egregious crimes perpetrated against children, and exclude, where feasible, these crimes from amnesty provisions and relevant legislation, and ensuring that post-conflict truth-and-reconciliation processes address serious abuses involving children."[120] It is with the resolution 1674 that the Security Council finally affirms that "mechanisms [of justice and reconciliation, including national, international and 'mixed' criminal courts and tribunals and truth and reconciliation commissions] may not only help to establish the individual responsibility for serious crimes, but also peace, truth, reconciliation and the rights of the victims."[121] This resolution reminds member states of their duty to fulfill their obligations to end impunity and to prosecute those responsible for war crimes, genocide, crimes against humanity, and gross violations of international humanitarian law. And, if these states do not have these legal institutions and independent national judicial systems, they need to take measures to build these institutions to give justice to the victims and to restore peace.

---

[119] CS Res. 1379, 20 November 2001, § 9 (a).

[120] Id.

[121] CS Res. 1674, 28 April 2006, § 7.

3.2 The child and the international rules of human rights

The international law of human rights seeks to promote compliance by member states in regard to civil and political rights as well as economic, social, and cultural rights of individuals or citizens. The rights are the legal recognition of human dignity and equality between people, and these rights are essential to the development of everyone. Even though human rights are not specifically written to protect people during armed conflicts, many of their articles are applicable in such cases.[122] Fundamental rights may be enshrined in documents designed specifically to protect them, whether at the universal level (the International Bill of Human Rights)[123] or regional level (American Convention on Human Rights)[124]. These same rights have their foundations in some thematic conventions, which may themselves be both universal and regional.[125]

3.2.1 The social and political rights of the child

The rights and freedoms and social policies for children are included in a single international convention. The Convention on the Rights of the Child, a convention of a universal theme, was adopted unanimously on November 20, 1989, by member states of the UN. This agreement, in the form of fifty-four articles, presents

---

[122] R. HARVEY, *op. cit.*, note 22, p. 8.

[123] Para. 1 and 6 (preamble), art. 2(1), 18 to 20 UDHR.

[124] Para. 2 (preamble), art. 1(1), 12, 13, 15 and 16.

[125] F. BOUCHET-SAULNIER, *op. cit.*, note 109, p. 157. *Cf.* Some examples of thematic conventions with a universal vocation of the United Nations (UN): the *Convention on the Prevention and Punishment of the Crime of Genocide,* the *Convention relating to the Status of Refugees,* and the *Optional Protocol to the Convention on the rights of the child with regard to the involvement of children in armed conflict*; see also examples of thematic regional conventions of the Organization of American States (OAS): the *Inter-American Convention against Terrorism* and the *Inter-American Convention against Corruption.*

the fundamental rights regarding the respect and the protection for each minor child. It stipulates that these rights must be implemented based on four principles: nondiscrimination, respect for the interests of the child, the right to survival and development, and the right to participation. Indeed, article 1 defines its scope by defining the word "child" as every human being below the age of eighteen years unless majority is reached early under the law that is applicable to him.

This definition seems to reflect the current debates on legal protection and the concept of child. Under this convention, state parties undertake to respect the rights set forth therein and to ensure that for each child living within their jurisdiction, their rights will be upheld without discrimination of any kind. These states must take all appropriate measures to ensure that the child is protected against all forms of discrimination or motivated punishment, and they must commit to ensure the child such protection and care necessary for his well-being.[126] In fact, article 32 protects children against economic exploitation and work that involve risks; article 40 protects the child suspect, to be accused or found of having infringed the penal law; and article 38 of the convention raises issues that directly relate to the use of children in armed conflict. Regarding the commitment of the states to respect and enforce all feasible measures to prevent children under fifteen not to participate directly in hostilities, under international humanitarian law, the same article requires states or governments who are signatories to refrain from recruiting into their armed forces all persons who are less than fifteen years of age and to protect the civilian population as well during armed conflicts.

On the other hand, the Optional Protocol to the Convention on the Rights of the Child on the Involvement of Children in Armed Conflicts reinforces the legal protection of children in helping

---

[126] Art. 2 and 3 CRC.

to prevent their use in armed conflicts.[127] But, can humanitarian law further strengthen its provisions against states that violate the convention? Who will or can prevent such states or rebel groups or paramilitary forces to recruit children into their armies? Although the Optional Protocol in its first article asks member states to take "all feasible measures," is it effective in protecting children's rights?

In fact, some believe that regional or transnational instruments are also designed to protect the rights of the child and to give children certain rights that are specific to their "cultural heritage, their history and values" of their civilization.[128] In regard to this statement, Africa—facing many conflicts—has become the continent that is the most ravaged by the scourge of recruitment and the riding of child soldiers. Leaders of that continent have been able to gather on July 9, 2002, several African governments in a regional organization called the African Union (AU). One of the goals of the AU is to "promote and protect human rights and peoples according to the African Charter on Human and Peoples' Rights."[129] In fact, nearly thirty-nine African countries have already ratified the African Charter, an agreement with a regional theme that includes provisions protecting civil and political rights and social, economic, and cultural needs of the African child. Inspired by other transnational and international instruments,[130] most of the rights contained in the African Charter are interpreted in the African context.

---

[127] Para. 6 and 11 (preamble) and art. 4 and 6.

[128] Para. 7 (preamble) ACRC.

[129] "About the AU," africa-union.org, 19 November 2006.

[130] Organization of African Unity (OAU), now called the African Union (AU), in July 1990, entered into force on November 29, 1999, after having received the ratification of fifteen states, the *African Charter on the Rights and Welfare of the Child,* which inspired the 1989 UN *Convention on the Rights of the Child,* the *Universal Declaration of Human Rights,* as well as the *Declaration on the Rights and Welfare of the African Child* (adopted by the OAU in July 1979), the *African Charter on Human and Peoples' Rights,* and the *Charter of the Organization of the African Union.*

Indeed, article 22 protects children in armed conflicts and prohibits their enlistment in the army. However, under the charter, "these provisions also apply to children in situations of internal armed conflicts,[131] tension and strife,"[132] terms that are not used in the Convention on the Rights of the Child of the UN. The African Charter, based on the administration of juvenile justice, contains provisions that protect children against economic exploitation[133] and obliges signatory states to give "special treatment" to the child who violates the criminal law.[134]

3.2.2   The rights and freedom of the child at work

The International Labor Law is a law that is part of the international law of human rights, especially regarding rights and social and economic freedoms. Indeed, every child is entitled to a standard of living adequate for its development.[135] Although parents are responsible, within their abilities and financial capacities, to ensure the development of the child,[136] it is important that the child is protected against economic exploitation.

---

[131] Armed conflicts or internal disturbances: these are de facto situations where there is an internal confrontation that presents a certain character of gravity or duration.

[132] Internal tensions or civil disturbances: these are less serious situations than those of internal disturbances. These are particularly situations of serious tension (political, religious, racial, ethnic, social, economic, etc.). These situations can precede or follow periods of conflict. In fact, according to the *Practical Dictionary of Humanitarian Law* (based on these two definitions mentioned), humanitarian law does not apply in situations where sporadic and isolated acts of violence and riots do not present a threshold of violence sufficient to talk about conflict and if they are not committed by an organized armed group capable of carrying out continuous and concerted operations.

[133] Art. 15, para. 1 CRC.

[134] *Id.*, art. 17, para. 1.

[135] Art. 27, para 1 CRC.

[136] *Id.*, para. 2.

However, when the child is forced to "work," which is to say to clear mines or do other dangerous work, he is entitled to enjoy his freedom and should not be performing any hazardous work or jeopardize his education or endanger his health or physical, mental, spiritual, moral, or social development.[137] In this regard, there are three important agreements with universal themes that have been adopted by the International Labor Organisation (ILO): Convention on the Abolition of Forced Labor,[138] Convention on the Worst Forms of Child Labor,[139] and the Convention on the Minimum Age.[140] Indeed, this last convention requires each state to commit to pursue a national policy to ensure the effective abolition of child labor and to raise progressively the minimum age for admission to employment or work.[141] Further, it requests that the minimum age for any employment that might endanger the health, safety, or morals of young persons should not be less than eighteen years.[142] In fact, the Convention on the Abolition of Forced Labor, itself considered the vanguard of the Convention on the Worst Forms of Child Labor, asks member states that have ratified it to commit to eliminate forced or compulsory labor and not to require it on any form.[143] Regarding the Convention on the Worst Forms of Child Labor, the same members must take immediate and effective measures to secure the prohibition and elimination of worst forms of child labor.[144]

---

[137] *Id.*, art. 32, para. 1.

[138] *Infra*, appendix (figure 2).

[139] *Id.*

[140] *Id.*

[141] Art. 1 C-138.

[142] *Id.*, art. 3, para. 1.

[143] Art. 1 C-105.

[144] Art. 1 C-182.

In this sense, the worst forms of child labor are defined as "all forms of slavery or practices similar to (...) including forced or compulsory recruitment of children for use in armed conflicts."[145] It is defined also as the use, procuring, or offering of a child for prostitution.[146] It's further defined as "the use, procuring or offering of a child for illicit activities, including production and trafficking of narcotics."[147] And, finally, it is any "works, in which, by its nature or circumstances it applies, are likely to harm the health, safety or morals of children."[148]

[145] *Id.*, art. 3 (a).

[146] *Id.*, art. 3 (b).

[147] *Id.*, art. 3 (c).

[148] *Id.*, art. 3 (d).

CHAPTER 4

International Law and the Paradoxical Status of Child Soldiers

International law does not exclude à priori the criminal responsibility of a child soldier who is accused of genocide, crimes against humanity, or war crimes,[149] for, if this was the case, why ask member states to "ensure that no child is suspected, accused or convicted of violating the penal law by reason of acts or omissions that were not prohibited by national or international law at the time those acts were committed"?[150] In fact, if international law refuses to charge child soldiers for "serious crimes," it is not only to avoid conflict with the national law[151] but also not to be responsible in managing the international system of juvenile delinquency. By taking charge of the administration of juvenile justice, international authorities would have to create an international tribunal of juvenile justice—with the same powers as those conferred on the International Criminal Court—to protect citizens of those countries that are members of the UN and to rehabilitate these youth for them to become responsible

---

[149] N. ARZOUMANIAN and F. PIZZUTELLI, *loc. cit.*, note 3, p. 843. *Cf.* In practice, it is likely that most children do not possess *mens rea* (the subjective element of the crime). The crime of genocide, for example, involves "the intention to destroy, in whole or in part, a national, ethnic, racial or religious group, as such" (*ICC Statute*, article 6). Is this the case for all children accused of genocide in Rwanda? *See* Chen REIS, "Trying the future, avenging the past: the implications of prosecuting children for participation in internal armed conflict," (1997) 28 <u>C.H.L.R</u>. 645.

[150] Art. 40 (2) (a) CRC.

[151] N. ARZOUMANIAN and F. PIZZUTELLI, *loc. cit.*, note 3, p. 827. *Supra*, note 108.

citizens in their communities, something that seems impossible for international law to do because of the costs that are associated with education and rehabilitation of children who are traumatized by the violence of armed conflicts. On a different level, what interests do the international authorities of member states that are rich and powerful have to create a juvenile court with powers to impose international sanctions on these third world young offenders in the form of rehabilitation and pardon?

Thus, the indeterminacy of international law over the legal status of child soldiers is especially evident in the paradox that the child soldier is both a victim and a perpetrator. International law wants to believe that the child cannot be an aggressor but rather a victim who deserves a form of "special treatment or protection." And, despite this "special protection," the child is left alone when the law is unable to meet his pressing needs considering he is already traumatized by the aftermath of the violence. By refusing to accept the child soldier as an aggressor, it is certain we will see an increase in juvenile delinquency in those countries with internal conflicts.

4.1 The child soldier and the legal system of juvenile delinquency

Everything happens as if international law reserves itself to protect the child soldier as a victim and return the treatment of the child soldier as an offender under the management of the juvenile justice system of each member state. In other words, international law leaves it to domestic law to administer juvenile justice under international standards that are established. These international standards are also drafted to enable countries to exercise broad discretion. For example, international law defines a "juvenile offender" as "a child or young person, accused or convicted of committing a crime,"[152] but

---

[152] Art. 2.2 (c) *Beijing Rules.*

nevertheless preserves the possibility for a country to declare that the criminal responsibility of a child not to be incurred until a certain age. In Canada's case, a juvenile offender is a child or young offender who is between twelve and seventeen years old. Children under twelve who commit what might be considered a criminal offense will not be tried for this crime but will likely be taken in charge by the support system for children at risk, known to Quebec under the term "protection system of youth."[153]

4.1.1 The concept of "juvenile delinquency"

The concept of juvenile delinquency is subjective according to the criteria of each country, based on the concept covering the behavior of juveniles who come under the provisions of their laws or penal codes, based on significant differences in terms of the system of penalties and based on differences in age of criminal responsibility of minors.[154] The two main objectives of the laws on juvenile delinquency[155] are the search for the *welfare* of the minor and state reactions toward juvenile delinquents, which should always be proportionate to the circumstances of offenders and offenses.[156] From these objectives, we have the "principle of proportionality," which serves to moderate the punitive sanctions, usually by referring them to the seriousness of the offense. In this sense, for a child soldier who

---

[153] *Loi modifiant la loi sur la protection de la jeunesse*, L.R.Q., c. P-34.1, art. 38(f) (2). *Infra*, appendix (figure 3).

[154] *Opinion of 9 May 2006 of the European Economic and Social Committee on the prevention of juvenile delinquency, methods of dealing with juvenile delinquency and the role of juvenile justice in the European Union*, OJ 2006 C 110/75.

[155] According to the definition provided by article 11(a) of the Annex to the *United Nations Rules for the Protection of Juveniles Deprived of their Liberty*, adopted on December 14, 1990, a minor is "any person under the age of 18" and that "the age below which it is forbidden to deprive a child of liberty is fixed by law."

[156] Art. 5.1 Beijing Rules.

commits a delinquent act [an offense if the act is committed by an adult], we must consider not only the severity of the act but also the personal circumstances to commit such act, such as social status, youth situation, damage caused by the act of delinquency, or other factors affecting personal circumstances.[157] International law also believes that those "legal systems that recognize the concept of threshold of criminal responsibility, it should not be set too low given the problems of emotional, psychological and intellectual maturity."[158] But, what can we say about those countries that do not recognize the threshold of criminal responsibility? What can we say when the seriousness of the delinquent act reaches or goes beyond the threshold of "serious crime"? Should we not consider the damage caused by this crime on victims—those victims who are maimed, tortured, raped, or killed? In fact, international law believes that states should ensure that children who are victims and witnesses have to have adequate access to judicial proceedings and are entitled to restitution and compensation for damage suffered.[159] This is true when one considers the impact of armed conflicts on children, "the importance of protecting children's rights in the operations of peacekeeping," and "problems children and young people are confronted as victims and perpetrators in situations of peace-building."[160]

In this context, the victims—be they children or adults—must participate in legal proceedings regarding their rights and double damages they suffer when international law ignores the criminal responsibility of the child soldier [aggressor] and when the law becomes faulty in the administration of juvenile justice. In fact,

---

[157] *Id.*, Commentary on Article 5.1, or *Principle of proportionality* as a second objective.

[158] *Id.*, art. 4.1 (*age of responsibility*). See appendix (figure 1).

[159] Title III, art. 43 (*Plans targeting children as victims and witnesses*). *Supra*, note 85.

[160] *Id.*, art. 29.

although states should establish juvenile courts, responsible primarily for "prosecuting juvenile offenders,"[161] one wonders how international law must justify its innovative recommendations[162] when his measures, it seems, have been developed for the protection of the child victim in the manner of Western culture and not to do justice to the child or the adult who is a victim and make the child soldier [aggressor] accountable for his crime.

4.1.2 The insurmountable dangers to the "socialization process"

International law recognizes that the prevention of juvenile delinquency is an essential element of crime prevention.[163] In fact, for us, one way to prevent crime is to accept the dual legal status of the child soldier. For international law, the socialization process of the different sectors of the population is another means of preventing delinquency. Certainly, one cannot ignore the contribution of society in this process, but can there be justice for the victims when the child is an abuser? Can the administration of juvenile justice operate with such impunity given to child soldiers? How can the state promote family cohesion and harmony in those countries that are still in conflict and, at the same time, discourage the separation of children from their parents[164] after the children have been recruited by force under the directives of the same states that are considered by international law as the main violators of human rights?

---

[161] *Id.*, art. 14 (d).

[162] *Id.*, art. 8, (Commentary in relation to the protection of privacy). According to international law, young people are particularly sensitive to criminal qualification, and they should not be qualified as "delinquents" or "criminals."

[163] Para. 1, (Basic Principles) *Guiding Principles* (Riyadh) *for the prevention of juvenile delinquency.* See AG Res. 45/112, 14 December 1990.

[164] *Id.*, art. 17.

Furthermore, how should nonprofit organizations that are dealing with youth receive financial aid and other benefits from the state and other institutions[165] when the state is bankrupt because of mismanagement and that the same state and other institutions [local and international] are using community organizations [operating supposedly as nonprofits with conditional grants] against their opponents? Also, how can the media encourage to provide young people access to information and documents from various national and international sources[166] when these media and journalists working as nonpartisans are often the targets of government or other armed groups? Finally, how should public bodies offer young people the opportunity to pursue full-time study and learn a trade[167] when these kids are both targeted by armed groups and politicized by the government and other sectors of the civil society who use them for their personal causes?

4.2 The child soldier and the weaknesses of international conventions

The power to punish these child soldiers, as we have seen it, is the responsibility of national courts. Therefore, the implementation of relevant international standards is dependent on the state and will be greatly diluted through various acts of reserves. Add to this the fact that the codification of the principles of international law may conflict with the custom of a country.

In fact, the African Charter on the Rights and Welfare of the Child states that member states of the African Union (AU) "must take into consideration the virtues of their cultural heritage, their history and values of African civilization which should inspire and

---

[165] *Id.*, art. 36.

[166] *Id.*, art. 40.

[167] *Id.*, art. 47.

guide their thinking on the rights and welfare of the child."[168] Further, the African Charter obliges member states to discourage "any culture, tradition, cultural or religious practice" that is "inconsistent with the rights, duties and obligations" outlined in the charter.[169] However, many believe that "the activity to give a written customary law does not confine itself to a work of a photographer reproducing the custom [the culture or tradition] as it is in its writing proposals."[170] Furthermore, although the codification of custom serves "to advance international law," the written form—according to some—"removes ambiguities and creates others."[171]

So, when customary law is threatened, "it may happen that the political circumstances block the ratification of these conventions by a large part of the international community."[172] There is also a false harmony of domestic law with international law when "the jurisdiction of the Court depends on the willingness of the parties" and that "the Court can exercise jurisdiction in respect of a State even if it is not with the latter's consent." Where the parties consent or express their will, they may be experiencing something else: the absolute refusal to initiate judicial proceedings against a warlord.

The ambiguous role of the International Court of Justice (ICJ) can be seen in its latent objectives with respect to the universal system of the United Nations for maintaining peace and international security, especially with their Commissions of Justice and Truth (CJT) and

---

[168] Para. 7 (preamble).

[169] Article 1.3.

[170] Tullio TREVES, "Harmony and Contradictions in the Codification of International Law," in Rafâa B. ACHOUR and Slim LAGHMANI (dir.), *Harmony and Contradictions in International Law*, Paris, Éditions A. Pedone, 1996, p. 79–85.

[171] *Id.*, p. 80.

[172] *Id.*, p. 83.

with their Disarmament, Demobilization, and Reintegration (DDR) programs.[173] While, on one side, the United Nations calls on parties in conflict to lay down their arms, sit at a negotiating table, and confess their sins, investigators of the court, on the other side, are armed with arrest warrants and seem to be actively looking for the main human rights abusers who are often sitting at the same negotiation tables. However, we wonder, are these violators actively sought after when they are protected by the same members of the peacekeeping mission who are sometimes officially part of the violators' security personnel?

4.2.1   The status of the child soldier in drafting of conventions

The rejection of the criminal responsibility of the child soldier under international law is based on article 26 of the Statute of the International Criminal Court, which declares that "the Court has no jurisdiction in respect of a person who was under 18 at the time of the alleged commission of a crime."[174] The wording of this article clearly demonstrates that the international protection systems contain several loopholes and weaknesses in the search for compromise in the rigor of the laid principles.

First, there is a search for compromise between the international legal systems and between the interests of different countries involved. In fact, the Geneva Convention[175] does not apply to noninternational conflicts except in article 3 of the four conventions, which obliges the parties of a noninternational conflict to guarantee a minimum protection for noncombatants. Despite the fact that this article applies to governmental and nongovernmental combatants, it is recognized

---

[173] Alain PELLET, "Harmony and Contradictions in International Justice," in R. B. ACHOUR and S. LAGHMANI (dir.), *op. cit.*, note 172, p. 197–202.

[174] *Supra*, note 11.

[175] *Supra*, note 6.

that article 3 is insufficient and cannot expose and regulate the growing number and nature of internal conflicts.[176] Furthermore, although the Protocol I to the Geneva Convention protects children against recruitment and involvement in armed conflicts, it allows children aged fifteen years and over to be recruited into armed forces or armed groups.[177] We may add that Protocol II of the Geneva Convention sets out minimum guarantees that the parties in a noninternational conflict must observed, but its rules are less severe against those who violate the protocol.[178]

Regarding the Convention on the Rights of the Child (CRC), one does not derogate in times of war or armed conflicts. However, the Committee on the Rights of Children, which is the CRC's control mechanism, "can not oversee the actions of actors in armed conflicts, make ad hoc recommendations and comment on the situations of countries that do not report."[179] In addition, the committee cannot hear individual complaints, disciplining or recommending compensation against violators.[180]

Another problem lies in the safeguards that temper the severity of the principles laid down in certain conventions.[181] Indeed, the

---

[176] R. HARVEY, *op. cit.*, note 22, p. 8.

[177] Art. 77, para. 2 Protocol I CG (*Protection of children*).

[178] Art. 6, para. 5 Protocol II CG (Calls on the authorities in power to grant "the widest possible amnesty," upon cessation of hostilities, to those who have taken part in the conflict. This recommendation may encourage impunity. It can be worse if these people are also the same authorities who are in violation of human rights).

[179] R. HARVEY, *op. cit.*, note 22, p. 12.

[180] *Id.*

[181] Hugues FULCHIRON, "International Conventions: Summary Presentation," in Jacqueline RUBELLIN-DEVICHI and Rainer FRANK (dir.), *The Child and International Conventions*, Lyon, Presses Universitaires, 1996, p. 19–33.

Optional Protocol to the Convention on the Rights of the Child on the Involvement of Children in Armed Conflict raises from fifteen to eighteen years of age at which participation in armed conflicts will be permitted and also prohibits the forcible recruitment of children under eighteen.[182] Nevertheless, this protocol is limited to the extent that it is optional and therefore dependent on the willingness of member states for ratification. It is also limited for the simple reason it does not prohibit indirect participation of children in armed conflicts[183] (this problem also arises with article 38 of the Convention on the Rights of the Child) and authorizes the recruitment of children under eighteen years on a voluntary basis and with parental consent.[184] Also, article 4 states that "only the government has the right to recruit, not guerrillas or paramilitary forces, children under 18 years of age and use them in armed conflicts."[185]

The use and involvement of children in acts of terrorism such as suicide bombers is another problem that international law has attempted to address as well. In fact, Ms. Pirkko Kourula, representative of the United Nations High Commissioner for Refugees (UNHCR), says that "girls were recruited to carry suicide bombs in Sri Lanka, as human shields in northern Uganda or as deminers in Iraq."[186] Regarding the case of Palestinian children, in a statement made by the Committee on Human Rights, Mr. Levy—representative of the state of Israel—said that young Palestinians are subjected to "paramilitary training and indoctrination in camps and summer school

---

[182] Art. 1 and 2 OP-CRC-AC.

[183] Art. 1. *Cf.* AG Res. 54/263, 29 August 2000.

[184] *Supra*, note 10. *Cf.* Article 3 requires that the child be informed about the duties attached to military service and that he provides proof of his age.

[185] *Id.*

[186] AG/SHC/428, 28 October 1999.

to become suicide bombers and martyrs."[187] During a special session
of the UN General Assembly on children,[188] two young Palestinian
delegates[189] have said that the child who is used as a "human bomb"
has the right to defend himself and that "we do not kill the innocent."
Although the Security Council has not directly addressed the problem
of children carrying a bomb in its resolution 1379, this resolution
is one of the most important resolutions on the need to protect
children against recruitment into armed groups. The same resolution
also attempts to link terrorism, armed conflicts, weapons, and drug
trafficking.[190] However, international law has never attempted or
agreed to define a child soldier who kidnaps, rapes, tortures, and kills
innocent people as an aggressor. International law, because of its lack
of jurisdiction before the International Criminal Court, is reluctant to
address the criminal liability of children who are involved voluntarily
in armed conflicts.

4.2.2   The status of the child soldier in the acceptance of conventions

The ambiguity of international law concerning the dual
legal status of the child soldier is evident not only in the drafting
of conventions but also in their reception. These conventions have
weaknesses both in their drafting and the approval, and these
weaknesses are found when a state can make reservations in respect

---

[187] CCPR/C/SR.2117, 9 October 2003.

[188] *Press conference on Palestinian children*, 10 May 2002.

[189] Jenin Zaal Abu Ruqti and Ahmad Khari, respectively fifteen and sixteen
years old.

[190] Art. 6 and 13(c). *See* CS Res. 1379, 20 November 2001. Yet the council
has never dared to clearly define the concept of "other criminal activity"
in the resolution. We must therefore rely on the texts of the International
Labor Organization (ILO) and, more particularly, article 3 of the Convention
on the Worst Forms of Child Labor, which defines the concept of "other
criminal activities" by the concept of "illicit activities," which are none other
than the production and trafficking of drugs.

of a convention at the time of its ratification, the interpretation of treaties, and the integration of these treaties into national law and, particularly the will of a state to enforce the agreement despite the ratification of those treaties by the authorities of that state.

In fact, the first problem that arises in the reception of international conventions by a signatory country provided that the state may issue a reservation in respect of a convention. States have the possibility of entering reservations to the application of certain articles of a convention. For example, El Salvador has made a statement about the sixteen-year-old Salvadoran children who are recruited into the army and said their recruitment is legal according to their national legislation on military service so that their law does not conflict with articles 2 and 6 of the Optional Protocol to the Convention on the Rights of the Child on the Involvement of Children in Armed Conflict.[191] This declaration allows El Salvador to "directly" use child soldiers in armed conflicts, which would violate article 1 of the protocol if they did not make that reservation. Worse yet, the reservation can be made unilaterally so that a state may remove, add, or change the meaning of a provision of a treaty because the state considers the treaty as an interference in its internal law. This is the case of Syria at the time of ratification of the Protocol on the Protection of Victims of International Armed Conflicts (Protocol I),[192] which said that ratification of the protocol "does not constitute an admission of Israel nor the establishment of relations with him regarding the provisions of that Protocol."[193] With this reservation, an Israeli soldier who is under eighteen at the time of conflict with Syria

---

[191] *Supra*, note 10. *Cf.* El Salvador ratified this protocol on April 18, 2002.

[192] *Supra*, note 7.

[193] *Notification of the Depositary to the ICRC*, 23 November 1983 (this same protocol was ratified by Syria on November 14, 1983).

can be arrested, tried, and sentenced to death for war crimes without Syria violating articles 4 and 5 of the said protocol.

The second problem is the interpretation of conventional treaties. In fact, the conventions were drafted to provide a solution to a problem and to give the member states the tools needed to solve its problem. The signatory state, which is probably the receiver party, must understand the definition and context of drafting of terms within this agreement. Otherwise, the agreement will be interpreted according to the culture and the legislation of the receiving country. This explains, partially at least, the [deliberate] ambiguity of international law over the legal status of child soldiers. The cultural values of a [Western] convention writer may indeed influence the drafting of a treaty with a thematic nature, which in turn will influence a receiver [let's say a Middle Eastern country] to interpret the same text based on his own culture, but not in the spirit of the rules of law and international instruments.

Third, the integration of these treaties in the legal systems of signatory countries is problematic. For example, in Pakistan, there are ordinances that are related to the Zina and Hadood[194] legislations that are not compatible with the principles and provisions of the Convention on the Rights of the Child (CRC). The latter results in a lack of consistency with national legislation regarding the definition of the child and the age of criminal responsibility, in those ordinances, which is too early.[195] Another problem related to the integration of those conventional treaties is the lack of human and material resources. In terms of human resources, the authorities who are concerned with the integration of these conventions into national legislation (usually

---

[194] Terms that correspond to the definition of the child.

[195] The age of criminal responsibility is seven years old in Pakistan. *Infra*, appendix (figures 3 and 4).

parliamentary members) must have the competence to understand and integrate these texts (technical and legal) into domestic law, which is not always the case. Regarding physical resources, the state must have the financial means to take charge of such legal reform and the publication of its laws, which, again, is far from certain.

Finally, we have a voluntarism problem. In fact, international law is based on voluntarism, which is to say all conventions and treaties are mostly signed and ratified according to the will of member states. But it happens that a signatory state to an agreement may simply refuse to implement it in its national legislation. For example, during the ratification of the Optional Protocol to the Convention on the Rights of the Child on the Involvement of Children in Armed Conflict[196] in November 2001, the Democratic Republic of Congo (DRC) stated, according to its national legislation,[197] no child under eighteen years of age would be an active member of the Congolese armed forces or other public or private armed groups working within the territory of the country. However, according to several sources, children continue to be used and recruited by armed groups who are in Congolese territory.[198]

Yet, if a state has voluntarily ratified an international convention, should that state—which includes human rights abusers, warlords, corrupt leaders, or gangsters working for the government—not be held responsible for violations of this convention? Indeed, the criminal responsibility should not be ignored when it comes to crimes against humanity when the state recruits, enlists, trains, arms, supplies,

---

[196] *Supra*, note 10.

[197] Law Decree No. 066 (June 9, 2000) on the *Demobilization and Rehabilitation of Vulnerable Groups*.

[198] "Congo DRC: New Violence in Kinshasa," Radio France Internationale, 21 November 2006.

involves, tolerates, and orders children to kill, torture, rape, and commit further acts of violence. But these children who kill, rape, and commit other unimaginable acts, what should we do with them? Should they not also be held accountable when they act voluntarily? Should we distinguish acts of child soldiers particularly from when those children act solely under order or only those acts that are committed by child soldiers when those children are considered victims and aggressors?

4.3 The paradoxical status of the child soldier during armed conflicts

The malaise of international law to consider the child soldiers as perpetrators is a calculated and deliberate conventional decision that is based on the legal concept that a child who is less than eighteen years old is a minor and cannot be responsible for his actions, and if he is, he must have a special treatment or protection. Isn't it a contradiction when a child can "voluntarily" enlist in the armed forces and participate "indirectly" in hostilities, while that same child soldier can rape, torture, and kill at will and still be accepted as a war victim because of armed conflicts? Isn't it a contradiction when a child working as a "commander" leads an armed group among which there are adults who lined up under his command and were ordered to torture and execute, and that same "commander" cannot even be tried for crimes against humanity because of his legal status as a child, a casualty of war, while those under his command—the foot soldiers—can be tried as war criminals?

Indeed, it is imperative that international law unambiguously decides on the dual status of the child soldier. It is imperative that this problem, which encourages not only the recruitment and systemic involvement of children in armed conflicts but also the systematic delinquency of children, is resolved in a clear and unequivocal manner.

In this regard, can the legal status of child soldiers be better defined by international law? In fact, who are those war victims? Don't those victims have the right to seek justice and compensation for acts committed against them? And, who are those aggressors? Can those perpetrators also become victims of war?

4.3.1   The child soldier or child victim

According to the Declaration of Basic Principles of Justice for Victims of Crime and Abuse of Power, a victim is one who has suffered harm because of an internationally wrongful act.[199] But, how can we tell whether the child soldier who is used and involved in armed conflicts is a victim of crime[200] or abuse of power[201]? In fact, there is no difference on this point because the member state recognizes in its national legislation that the conscription of children is illegal,[202] and the international law stipulates that the recruitment and the use of children in hostilities may constitute a war crime.[203]

---

[199] AG Res. 40/34, 29 November 1985.

[200] *Id.* A victim of crime is defined as a person or a group of persons who, individually or collectively, have suffered harm, in particular injury to their physical or mental integrity, moral suffering, material loss, or serious violation of their fundamental rights because of acts or omissions that "infringe the criminal laws in force in a Member State, including those which proscribe criminal abuse of power" (cf. part A, art. 1 on *Victims of Crime*).

[201] *Id.* defines when a person or a group of persons, individually or collectively, have suffered harm, in particular an attack on their physical or mental integrity, moral suffering, material loss, or a serious violation of their fundamental rights because of acts or omissions that "do not yet constitute a violation of national criminal law, but which represent violations of internationally recognized human rights standards" (*cf.* part B, art. 18 on *Victims of Abuse Power*).

[202] *Supra,* note 199.

[203] *Supra,* notes 11, 12 and 13. *Cf.* Second paragraph of the introduction.

However, the child soldier who is used for sexual purposes, forced to join an armed group, or executed under suspicion of conspiracy or for refusing to fight is considered a victim of crime and/or abuse of power. Indeed, it was found during the last decade that more than 2 million children have been killed in armed conflicts, more than 4.5 million have been rendered disabled, and more than 30 million have been taken by force from their homes not to mention those thousands of young women who have been subjected to sexual abuse.[204] This means that children are increasingly becoming the target of barbaric acts, both as victims of horrific crimes as well as mere objects in the hands of adults who train them to commit atrocities.[205] In fact, according to Carol Bellamy, executive director of the United Children's Fund (UNICEF), the creation of the International Criminal Court (ICC) appear indeed as "a clear signal that atrocities committed against children will not go unpunished and those responsible for acts of torture, rapes, murders and disappearances of children will be brought to justice." However, what will we do of these children, such as Kay Yussuf, who commit many barbaric acts and atrocities,[206] and about Patrick, a thirteen-year-old child from Uganda, who was forced to kill his own mother to be enlisted in the guerrilla force of Joseph Kony, the leader of the Lord's Resistance Army (LRA)?[207]

---

[204] Olara OTUNNUN, Special Representative of the UN Secretary General on the Impact of Armed Conflict on Children. *Infra*, appendix (figure 2).

[205] THE UNITED CHILDREN'S FUND, *The state of the world's children in 2005: Childhood under threat*, New York, Unicef House, 2004, 39–65.

[206] Kay Yussuf, a child soldier from Liberia who was under sixteen when he committed criminal acts, said, "If I have committed a lot of atrocities such as rape, murder, cut off arms, feet, the ears, it wasn't my fault; but, it is because of the war; for, it was not my wish to participate in the atrocity!" *Supra*, note 27, Murdered Childhood.

[207] *Supra*, note 20.

4.3.2 The victims of child soldiers

A war victim is defined as any person [child or adult, man or woman] that international humanitarian law seeks to protect and who is affected by the effects of armed conflicts. Any person [child or adult, man or woman, who suffered an international or noninternational armed conflict] is entitled to an effective remedy before competent national [and international] courts against acts that violate the fundamental rights that are granted under the national constitution or international law.[208]

These victims, who are usually victims of abuse of power,[209] are often subject to criminal and barbaric acts such as kidnapping, hostage taking, torture, and murder. There is also the mass rape of women or the policy of systematic rape as part of a war strategy to intimidate the population. According to human rights workers who have experimented firsthand those atrocities in the war zones, because of this indiscriminate violence and acts of sexual assault, thousands of women are infected with the AIDS virus.[210] And much of the sexual violence are committed by child soldiers, known as *kadogos* or "the little things of nothing" or simply "destroyers of vaginas" and "vagina snatchers."[211] Many of these victims, who are over ten million worldwide, have suffered severe psychological trauma.[212] In fact, according to many, "there is no weaker or more vulnerable than a woman forced into a corner by child soldiers who use rape as the most effective weapon."[213]

---

[208] Art. 8 UDHR.

[209] *Supra*, note 203.

[210] *Supra*, note 89.

[211] BOLYA, *op. cit.*, note 78, p. 85.

[212] O. OTUNNUN, *loc. cit.*, note 65, 69.

[213] *Supra*, note 30.

In ruling on the victims' rights, international law gives legal protection to war victims.[214] According to a decision of the International Criminal Court (ICC), victims have the right to participate in the procedural stage of an investigation that concerns them. In addition to this protection, the International Criminal Court (ICC) expands victims' rights by guaranteeing those victims the right to defense and the right to get the necessary protection. Thus, these victims are entitled to present their general views and concerns on a crime investigation that is committed during armed conflicts, and they have also the right to participate in the fight against impunity.[215]

4.3.3   The child soldier or child aggressor

During armed conflict, a child soldier can be an abuser when he directs or orders, as agent for the government, the planning or the initiation of an attack against a certain group or a population to claim victims or take prisoners.[216] These children can become real abusers who voluntarily commit serious crimes either as commanders or just to be promoted to a higher rank.[217] In this case, the child plays the leading role of a strategist when he—because of his military status in the guerrilla, paramilitary forces, rebel army, or regular army—commands an armed group.[218]

In fact, international humanitarian law considers the hierarchical nature of the armed forces and discipline that is being enforced by commanders, and it imposes on commanders specific obligations while engaging their individual criminal responsibility in certain

---

[214] *Supra*, note 210.

[215] **ICC–01/04–101,** 17 January 2006.

[216] Section 1.2.2 CIDA. *Cf.* Definition of the concept of child aggressor.

[217] C. KEITESI, *op. cit.*, note 28, p. 101.

[218] R. HARVEY, *op. cit.*, note 22, p. 51.

circumstances. Humanitarian law establishes criminal responsibility of commanders who give orders to their subordinates who violate humanitarian law and leave their subordinates the opportunity to commit crimes, not taking sanctions against subordinates who violate humanitarian law on their own initiative despite that they are unaware that these violations are taking place.[219] Regardless of the commander's responsibility, the individual who receives orders also has an obligation under international humanitarian law. So anyone (child or adult, commander or others) who commits a crime shall be personally and criminally responsible for his actions.[220]

4.3.4   The aggressors of child soldiers

One can never ignore that children can be manipulated to commit horrible crimes. Those warlords and their associates who exploit and use children to carry their personal ambitions must necessarily respond to the violations of international humanitarian law and human rights, which require warlords not to recruit, utilize, and involve children in armed conflicts. In fact, forcing a nonwilling child to participate in criminal acts is a form of crime against humanity. Although children may be abusers themselves, it is very important for governments to have the will to enact and enforce national legislation that prohibits the abuse and the exploitation of children and young people as well as laws that protect those children from being used to commit crimes.[221] The international community has a great responsibility and must also be willing to arrest and try those warlords, but they should not want

---

[219] Art. 49 CG I and II; art. 129 CG III; art. 146 CG IV; art. 86.2 Protocol I CG.

[220] Art. 3, Haye Convention (1907); art. 49 CG I; art. 50 CG II; art. 129 CG III; art. 146 CG IV; art. 75.4 (b), 86, 87 Protocol I CG. *Cf.* Art. 25 (a), (c) et (i) SR-CPI.

[221] Art. 53 PDR.

to appease those criminals for reasons that are often beyond their decision to bring justice to victims.

4.4 The nonparadoxical status of the child soldier following armed conflicts

There is no doubt, during an armed conflict, international law regards child soldiers as victims even if they commit serious crimes. In the view of the law, these children should not be held responsible either once these conflicts are over.[222] Indeed, criminal responsibility simply does not exist for these children during or after armed conflicts; according to international law, this matter should be the responsibility of member states that legislate a national policy or domestic law. Whereas, national state orders can only be sensitive to the pressures of international law that views a child aggressor as a victim. In fact, under a strong influence of international law, domestic law naturally succumbs to the desire of seeing the aggressor becoming the victim, especially when its judicial system is failing. It is common that because of a lack of human and material resources, the member state is not able to handle problems that fall in the wake of an armed conflict: corruption, drug trafficking, and a lack of democratic experience. These problems perpetuate the failure of law and, thus, become obstacles to rebuilding the rule of law, securing justice for victims, disarming, demobilizing, reintegrating, and rehabilitating these children and veteran soldiers.

We wonder if international law is truly concerned about the satisfaction rate of those victims who are child soldiers as well as the victims of child soldiers. What about the satisfaction rate for aggressors who, for the most part, are child soldiers? In fact, to promote peace and reconciliation, international actors in the UN Security Council

---

[222] Art. 26 SR-CPI.

seem to opt for impunity[223] while forgetting the purpose of resolution 1674, which underlines that "states have the obligation to end impunity and prosecute those responsible for crimes of genocide, war crimes, ethnic cleansing and crimes against humanity."[224] Thus, the satisfaction of seeing the truth known in the open and encouraging victims to exercise their most basic rights is under threat: first, the victims cannot obtain justice; and, second, the aggressors are rewarded.

4.4.1   The child soldiers: victims or aggressors

During armed conflicts, child soldiers who are victims of crime or abuse of authority[225] by warlords will also make their own victims. After these armed conflicts, those victims are also entitled to "access to judicial proceedings and to prompt redress for the harm they suffered as envisaged by national law" or international law.[226] Those who commit criminal acts—namely, the aggressors—"must make fair restitution to victims, their families or their dependents."[227] Considering these requirements, we must recognize that millions of

---

[223] F. BOUCHET-SAULNIER, *op. cit.*, note 109, p. 268. *Cf.* Aggressors and violators of international norms are often granted immunity with reservations that are based on specific conditions. For us, this immunity—which grants violators the benefits of avoiding prosecution—encourages impunity that can result from a dysfunction or disappearance of the justice system. Also, in international law, impunity stems mainly from the absence of a judicial apparatus capable of judging breaches of established rules. It is the national courts that most often assume the criminal sanction of crimes. Further, war crimes or crimes against humanity that are committed by state officials or under their command during periods of armed conflict are therefore particularly difficult to repress.

[224] CS Res. 1674, 28 April 2006, § 8.

[225] *Supra*, note 197; *id.*, note 198.

[226] Art. 4, AG Res. 40/34, 29 November 1985 (*cf.* Access to justice and fair treatment).

[227] *Id.*, art. 8 (*Obligation of restitution and reparation*).

children and adults "around the world suffer harm from crime and abuse of power" and that these children and adults, "whose rights have not been adequately recognized, may suffer further harm in the process of justice."[228]

Indeed, despite these legal provisions and statutory international law, the international legal community prefers not to refer the child soldier to an international tribunal, but rather to a domestic tribunal to be tried and sentenced. In fact, after the genocide in Rwanda, more than 4,454 former child combatants were arrested for genocide and crimes against humanity after the organization of the Gacaca,[229] a form of participatory and popular justice system with the sole mission to try "serious crimes." In this type of judiciary system, accused children were classified according to the seriousness of the offenses, and their sentences were reduced.[230] However, although this system seems to work for the victims of genocide, we can see two problems: first, there is "no procedural safeguards" for those children who are placed in rehabilitation centers; and, second, those who were serving their sentences "are undergoing the same procedure as adults."[231]

For international law, the best way to help these children, once cruel, barbaric, and inhuman, is not to call them to testify in court. In fact, the representative of the United Nations Children's Fund (UNICEF) in Freetown (Sierra Leone), despite the fact that she recognizes that these "small soldiers" are guilty, believes that "by putting these children before a Special Court would be considered

---

[228] *Supra*, note 154.

[229] Literally means "grass" in the Kinyarwanda language. This judicial system is created by article 2 of the Organic Law No. 40/2000, which, according to article 74(1), recognizes the age of fourteen as the age of criminal responsibility at the time of the offense (*supra*, note 3).

[230] N. ARZOUMANIAN and F. PIZZUTELLI, *loc. cit.*, note 3, p. 848.

[231] *Id.*

another punishment based on the fact that they are primarily victims [of armed conflicts]."[232] She continues to say that if the United Nations (UN) took the decision to prosecute child soldiers, she would not dare imagine what awaits these children.[233] David Crame, the prosecutor of the Special Court for Sierra Leone (SCSL), declared that children who are less than eighteen years old will not be brought or tried, but he will ensure "those who are forcing children to commit horrendous crimes" will be judged.[234]

Considering the mindset of official representatives of international law in regard to authors and actors of armed conflicts, what kind of messages are they sending to victims of these conflicts that sometimes end in genocide? What kind of messages are they sending also to actors and authors of these conflicts? What can we say about the Hutu youth who came with sticks known as *cocomacac* and machetes to eliminate a generation of Tutsis? What can we say about these young militiamen who, in their plan to kill the survivors, took the little children by their legs and knocked them on the wall?[235] One may wonder what might really happen to these child soldiers if these children [aggressors] were to appear before an international court for juvenile.

4.4.2   The aggressors: child soldiers and warlords

In June 2004, the Court of Appeals for the Special Court for Sierra Leone (SCSL) handed down a landmark decision holding that the recruitment of children who are less than fifteen years old is a

---

[232] Roch SONNET, "Johana Van Guerten: No child soldiers at the helm. Judge child soldiers?" Afrik.com, October 13, 2000.

[233] *Id*.

[234] R. HARVEY, *op. cit.*, note 22, p. 80.

[235] *Supra*, note 24. *Cf.* Testimonies of Louis Rutaganira, a Tutsi trader.

war crime under customary international law.[236] The same court also had three options to try former child combatants: "keep criminal responsibility for 18 years old youth, establish a truth commission and submit these children, based on a judicial proceeding, to a court that respects international standards of juvenile justice."[237] The last option was selected under strong pressure from the civil society and members of government, which would allow the Special Court for Sierra Leone (SCSL) to be the first international court to try child soldiers for crimes of genocide and crimes against humanity.[238] However, as it was predicted considering the international community's usual plan toward poor countries with armed conflict, David Crane, prosecutor of the tribunal, refused the third option despite the court now can bring to justice, according to the seriousness of their crimes, fifteen-to-eighteen-year-old children.[239]

In spite of it all, we can say that the jurisprudence of the Special Court for Sierra Leone (SCSL), in regard to convictions against recruiters of child soldiers, has a positive impact on recruitment and involvement of children in future armed conflicts, although this particular problem was not the direct result of these convictions.[240] In fact, Thomas Lubanga became the first warlord to be accused of war crimes for the recruitment and the use of child soldiers, on a

---

[236] *Prosecutor v. Sam Hinga Norman*, SCSL-2004-14-AR72 (E), 31 May 2004.

[237] N. ARZOUMANIAN and F. PIZZUTELLI, *loc. cit.*, note 3, p. 852.

[238] *Id.* (*Cf.* S/2000/915, 4 October 2000). To try child soldiers [aggressors], the report replaced the expression "those who bear the greatest responsibility" in *resolution* 1315 of 14 August 2000 (see para. 3) with the expression "who are mainly responsible" (see part C, para. 29 of the report on *Competence ratione personae*).

[239] R. HARVEY, *op. cit.*, note 22, p. 80.

[240] The International Criminal Tribunal for Rwanda rendered four judgments in the cases against Clément Kayishema, Obed Ruzindana, Omar Serushago, Jean-Paul Akayesu, and Jean Kambanda for genocide and crimes against humanity between September 1998 and May 1999.

large scale, in hostilities.[241] After the confirmation of charges against Lubanga,[242] in a first hearing, Luis Moreno-Ocampo—the prosecutor of the International Criminal Court (ICC)—stated that the court was conducting investigations in Darfur and that arrest warrants had already been issued against Joseph Kony[243] and his lieutenants, settled in northern Uganda, for war crimes and for recruiting and conscripting child soldiers in armed conflicts.[244] Despite this progress of the International Criminal Court (ICC) and other special courts, there is an almost systematic offer of immunity by international actors to warlords, violators of international humanitarian law and human rights. This immunity, which can be describe as impunity, comes usually in the form of Truth and Reconciliation Commission (TRC) and the program of Disarmament, Demobilization, and Reintegration (DDR) of the United Nations (UN). However, the Convention on the Rights of the Child (CRC) states that "the State must take measures to promote physical and psychological recovery and social reintegration of children who are victims of any form of neglect, exploitation or abuse, torture, or any form of cruel, inhuman, or degrading treatment, or armed conflict."[245]

Whereas, these programs become an official pass for the main perpetrators to enjoy impunity. Indeed, the mandate of those truth commissions is not based on a quest for justice, but rather "to explore the fullness of experience" of these aggressors to "understand their

---

[241] *Supra*, note 58. See also note 59.

[242] *The Prosecutor v. Thomas Lubanga Dyilo*, ICC-01/04-01/06, November 9, 2006. *Cf.* After a preliminary hearing in September 2007, the court and the defense agree for the trial to begin on March 31, 2008.

[243] *Supra*, note 20.

[244] *Opening Remarks: Fifth Session of the Assembly of State Parties*, The Hague, 23 November 2006.

[245] Art. 39 CRC.

motivations."[246] These commissions do not seek either to explore the guilt of those children but to "examine their role as aggressors" "to prevent future conflicts."[247] How can these commissions prevent future conflicts when these children who are psychologically traumatized find themselves offered a general amnesty without being integrated into a rehabilitation program? In fact, the Justice and Peace Commission of the Democratic Republic of Congo (DRC) did not take any action to help these children.[248] And, what can we say about the disarmament program of the United Nations (UN)?

The Disarmament, Demobilization, and Reintegration (DDR) program also continues to offer large-scale of impunity. For example, at one point, Kyungu Mutanga Gideon—commander of the terrible and feared Mai Mai militia—was the most wanted man by the United Nations Mission in Congo (MONUC) for war crimes and for recruiting and conscripting child soldiers in armed conflicts. However, this warlord was likely to be appointed commander in the Congolese army on condition that he stops the killings.[249] In the province of Bunia, Democratic Republic of Congo (DRC), the two main rebel groups[250] agreed to disarm in exchange for amnesty and positions in government armed forces following a peace agreement initiated by the UN since 2002. Fortunately, on March 5, 2009, Gedeon was found guilty by a DRC military tribunal for crimes against humanity and was sentenced to death.

---

[246] SIERRA LEONE TRUTH AND RECONCILIATION COMMISSION, *Witness to truth: Children and the Armed Conflict, Report 2002-2006*, Freetown, Truth and Reconciliation Commission, 2006, p. 232–338.

[247] *Id.*, p. 286, para. 225.

[248] N. ARZOUMANIAN and F. PIZZUTELLI, *loc. cit.*, note 3, p. 847.

[249] Juliette L. DORÉ and Anneke V. WOUDENBERG, "The Congo cannot condone the impunity of warlords," Human Rights Watch, 19 November 2006.

[250] Revolutionary Movement of Congo and Matate de Cobra.

On the other hand, under the dicta of the United Nations Mission for Stabilization in Haiti (MINUSTAH), the Haitian government established the National Commission for Disarmament, Demobilization, and Reintegration (NCDDR). However, more than US $40 million are already used in this program without a real success because the *chimères*, members of armed groups, trying to gain time. Ultimately, the government—to appease his supporters (chimères)—decided to appoint Jean-Baptiste Jean Philippe, alias Samba Boukman, as a member of the Committee on Disarmament. In fact, Samba Boukman was the spokesperson for Operation Baghdad, which was an armed movement that killed more than 1,939 people, among them 108 policemen, 10 peacekeepers, and 4 journalists.[251] According to Anneke Van Woudenberg, senior researcher at Human Rights Watch, this type of agreement cannot bring anything good. One can easily foresee a rebel, wanting to become a colonel, decided to take up arms and start killing people.[252]

Indeed, the warlords only see themselves because of their personal ambitions. And, when they mobilize their deadly force, it is always in the name of the people or in the name of democracy. They do not realize that "when ordering child soldiers to kill, they trigger a series of psychological reactions"[253] among those children who cannot find the help they need, especially when their dual legal status remains ambiguous. In fact, Jan Egeland, Undersecretary General for Humanitarian Affairs, suggested to the Security Council to transform resolution 1674 into a real platform for action to end the suffering.[254]

---

[251] *Press release: Concern of the RNDDH in the face of escalating slippages in the management of State affairs, National Human Rights Defense Network (RNDDH),* 19 September 2006.

[252] "Congo's holdout militias agree to disarm," CNN.com, 27 July 2006.

[253] *Supra,* note 30.

[254] "Turning resolution 1674 into a platform for action, asks Jan Egeland," UN

He wants the Security Council to agree more systematically in situations of crises, to maintain peace operations that are more integrated, to strengthen its humanitarian response, and to put in place in many member states more effective legal remedies. He believes that the peacekeepers are not trained to meet the challenges posed by the "Young Patriots" who resort to street violence and crime. One wonders what the real objective of the United Nations is in a country like Haiti, where thousands of young children who are living in poor neighborhoods decide to be recruited by wolves dressed as monks to silence the weapon of dialectic by the dialectic of weapons.

News Center, 29 June 2006.

PART III

The International Community's Responses to Armed Conflicts and Their Susceptibility to Bring Antagonistic Solutions to the Problems of Child Soldiers: The Case of Haiti

CHAPTER 5

Genesis and Evolution of the "Civil War" in Haiti: An Open Debate

The evolution of the chaotic situation in Ayiti[255] goes way back and, particularly, since the landing of Christopher Columbus, in December 1492, in this enchanted island where 1.1 million Indians live. The Spaniards, by their greed and based on their need for labor, forced the original inhabitants of the island to work days and nights in gold mines. In the space of only twenty years, in 1516, only sixteen thousand Indians are numbered all over the territory! Before this genocide, the Jesuit priest Bartolome de Las Casas—well known as the "Protector of the Indians"—presented to the Spanish authorities his "Memoire of Fourteen Remedies" in which he advocated not only the end of forced labor for the Indians but also the kidnapping of blacks from Africa who will be put on the path for slavery in the New World to offset the mortality of the natives. Following his lobbying for the Indians to Queen Isabella, in less than ten years, more than nine thousand blacks were brought from Africa, marking the beginning of the slave trade throughout the Americas.

Strangers in the New World and away from their familial and natural environment, these giant and strong Africans, and also very young, will not remain docile for too long. Several escapes, escape attempts, and a few fires on plantations and other properties are

---

[255] Means in Indian language (Tainos) "land of high mountains"; also called *Hispaniola* (little land of Spain) by the Spaniards and *Santo Domingo* by the French.

recorded. Worse, with the arrival of the French—new masters of the New World—those escapees are becoming increasingly organized to combat slavery. In fact, starting in 1702, the "marronnage"[256] allows slaves to maintain both their warrior tradition and gain proficiency in weapons handling. It is probably during those escapes that children were recruited as soldiers for the first time in the American continent. In fact, a group of *marrons* can be between 1,500 and 2,000 armed men and children.[257] Depending on the extent of the movement, several groups can be joined together after a mutual agreement. During the month of April 1798, Toussaint became the leader of the Congos,[258] and he is now ready to fight against the French commissioner Gabriel Hedouville, a Gironde, which has a secret mission from Gen. Napoleon Bonaparte to restore slavery on the island.[259] In fact, in a letter addressed to General Bonaparte, one can see General Leclerc's foreseeability and carefulness toward the French policy with regard to Haiti: "In order to restore slavery and crush the revolution, we should exterminate all blacks living in the mountains, women and men, except for children under 12 years old!"[260]

Indeed, there were plenty of good reasons for the French to be scared of these older children because some of them had the chance to participate in international conflicts. For example, on September

---

[256] A form of guerrilla warfare; one of the first leaders was François Macandal— originally from Guinea—during the era of slavery.

[257] Robert D. HEINL and Nancy G. HEINL, "Written in Blood—The Story of the Haitian People: 1492-1971," Boston, Houghton Mifflin Company, 1978, p. 29.

[258] A group of twenty thousand armed men and children with Congolese roots.

[259] Léger-Félicité Sonthonax, a French Jacobin commissioner (antislavery), abolished slavery by a decree, which was published on August 29, 1793.

[260] R. HEINL and N. HEINL, *loc. cit.*, note 257, p. 170. It should also be noted that General Leclerc is very open about the status of children who were over twelve years old. According to him, these children are dangerous because they are trained, armed, and well equipped.

8, 1779, Henry Christopher (a boy of twelve years old and future colonial army general),[261] Jean Pierre Boyer (aged sixteen and future president), and other leaders of the revolution were part of a battalion of more than five hundred men and boys who called themselves "Chasseurs Volontaires from Saint-Domingue." This armed group, under the command of French general Charles d'Estaing, was to participate in the American War of Independence against the British while providing support, in the city of Savannah (Georgia), to the four thousand American soldiers who were placed under the command of Maj. Gen. Benjamin Lincoln.

Other children who did not participate in the war of Savannah have acquired their war experiences on the battlefield with armed gangs who fight against the slave system. For example, after the death of the voodoo priest Boukman—one of the leaders of the marrons—Jeannot became the leader of more than six thousand armed men, including children who are less than twelve years old. In August 1791, this insurgent group was armed with guns, knives, sticks, spears, and all sorts of kitchen utensils and farm or sharp objects.[262] Then they killed men, raped their women, and set fire to their homes.[263]

For the Spaniards and the French, they were able to control the insurgency with their powerful weapons. Indeed, several marron leaders had their heads cut off, and their severed heads were placed on poles, which were aligned along the trail, as a sign of warning to future insurgents.[264] Following this threat, the marron leaders

---

[261] Considered, because of his notoriety, as the first Haitian child soldier; he was drafted into the American Independence War as a drummer.

[262] R. HEINL and N. HEINL, *loc. cit.*, note 257, p. 29.

[263] Note that both Spaniards and French also raped black women while acting with cruelty against men. These rapes thus contributed to a new social class of men and women, who are called half-breeds or mulattoes.

[264] Over one thousand plantations were destroyed, and ten thousand insurgent

have realized that they must eventually comply by either joining the Spaniards or the French—which were two mortal enemies[265]—to be trained and be better equipped with weaponry. Aside from these war experiences, some "Chasseurs Volontaires" and other notorious leaders of armed groups, such as Toussaint, Jean-François and Biassou, became double agents working on behalf of the French and Spanish authorities.

5.1   The violence in Haiti

On January 1, 1804, after several heroic struggles against the French troops, Gen. Jean-Jacques Dessalines—the new leader[266] of the native army and other armed groups—declared Haiti an independent country. Nevertheless, some say that Haiti was like "a powder keg that the slightest spark could explode!" A few weeks later, there came the executions in public squares of major cities: children, armed with swords and daggers, began to cut the throats of the traitors and their former masters.

From 1804 until today, Haiti is experiencing a succession of ephemeral governments after being succumbed by civil wars and internal tensions. Even the father of the Haitian independence was not immune to this violence. Indeed, on October 17, 1806, Dessalines—who was accused of tyranny and making unbearable agrarian policy—was murdered in a plot that was set up by his trusted former child

---

slaves lost their lives.

[265] These two colonial powers, and even the British, were fighting among themselves to control the island.

[266] Governor-General Toussaint Louverture, suspected of conspiracy and rebellion, was arrested by French forces and died in captivity on April 8, 1803, at Fort de Joux, France. His death left the leadership of the revolution to the black general Jean-Jacques Dessalines.

soldiers and war companions.[267] In 1807, the country was now divided into two republics: the Western Republic (led by Alexandre Petion, a mulatto) and the Northern Republic (led by Henri Christophe, a black and a former child soldier in the war of Savannah).[268] In April 1844, Louis Jean-Jacques Accau—a former member of the armed group the Congos—became the leader of the armed group, which was known as the Armée Souffrante (Suffering Army). His group, armed with machetes, some rusty guns, and spears, was composed of two thousand farmers (adults and children) who inhabited the hills and valleys of Camp Perrin. The objectives of the group, now called the Piquets (stakes), were to overthrow the government of Riviere Herard and seize property and other valuable possessions. To prevent the Piquets armed group to achieve their goals, the government asked Col. Faustin Soulouque—a former child soldier in the Haitian revolutionary army—to form and lead an armed group with his supporters who lived in the western part of the country. Following the order, Soulouque formed a loyal armed gang for the president of Haiti, and it was called the Zinglins (name taken from small pieces of broken bottles that stuck to your feet if you walk barefooted), who became the ugly bane for the Piquets. The northern insurgents, for their part, under the leadership of Nissage Saget, organized their own armed group—the Cacos—as an opposition for the Piquets and the Zinglins. In February 1869, young people—who were between fourteen and seventeen years old and members of the armed group the Piquets—have besieged the prison located in the city of Les Cayes, where they made a real carnage!

---

[267] One of his collaborators is Henri Christophe, a former child soldier. *Supra*, note 261.

[268] The western republic has an army of 22,200 soldiers, and the one from the northern part of the island has an army of 19,400 soldiers.

It is important to mention that a Haitian child soldier, even during the colonial era, does not become a voluntary member of an armed group. Very often, the child was forced to join the rebellion. The most vivid description of a forced recruitment of the child soldier is based on a testimony of an American diplomat during the civil war of 1868: "Recruitment has always been done by group and by the strength of the stick, in mountainous areas, they [new recruits] are pushed like wild animals and brought in cities like cattle with their legs tied with a rope long enough to allow them to walk with their arms tied behind them. These people are from 14 to 65 years old. If some are resisting or trying to escape, they were shot as they fled."[269] Fifty years later, the same forms of recruitment continued. Indeed, in March 1910, Haitian president Antoine Simon ordered his officers to go into the fields, in streets, and into houses during the day as well as at night to capture men and children. Every two days, the general in charge of the forced recruitment sent the young recruits to Port-au-Prince to be trained and to become soldiers who will fight insurgents. The older ones were penalized by being forced to pay their recruitment fees according to their economic means.[270] Meanwhile, the government wanted to improve the conditions of the population. Unfortunately, the president—sometimes a civilian—came to collide with the traditional position of the army who always still refused to implement reforms. For example, to counter the military, Pres. Antoine Simon decided to include members of the armed group Zinglins within his government under the official and public service name of Service of Homeland Security. Thus, Zinglins—who were former gang members—became officially the new members of the secret police. In April 1915, the government of Guillaume Sam was facing a rebellion of the Cacos

---

[269] R. HEINL and N. HEINL, *loc. cit.*, note 257, p. 327. See also appendix (figure 6).

[270] *Id.*, p. 360.

in the north. And, to counter these revolts and maintain his army, he used the same methods of recruitment from his predecessors. Recruiters started to go door to door, from village to village, beating the young boys and children—after they were tied up with ropes—to force them to join the army of Guillaume Sam.

However, with the US occupation in July 1915, the indigenous army and other security forces were destabilized. In fact, before the occupation, the Haitian Armed Forces had 9,000 soldiers, including 308 generals, 50 colonels, and lower ranks. During the occupation, as for February 1916, the United States created a police force within the Haitian population, which had a total of 1,500 men to secure the country.[271] In June 1916, the number increased by 2,553 troops, including 115 American officers. However, many ex-combatants from different armed groups were integrated into the new police force. In September 1919, there were over 131 attacks by members of the armed groups who were not recruited in the new force. These attacks were focused against both the new Haitian police and the US Marines. The Cacos, for the most part, claimed of being the mastermind behind these attacks. Already regarded as nationalists, they were very spirited, and they used the techniques of guerrilla warfare. Thus, Charlemagne Peralte, a former child soldier who, at the age of twenty-two, became the leader of the Cacos, was the most dangerous and the most wanted man on Haitian soil. Finally, he was betrayed by one of his fighting companions who did not like his policy against the Americans. Finally, members of the US Marines exposed his bruised body in the public square for several days as a way to stop rebellions against the US occupation. Despite that the occupation has ended several years later, the uprisings and revolts continued for the worse. But before their departure in 1934, the Americans established the Military School,

---

[271] Article X, *Convention between the Republic of Haiti and the United States of America*, 17 September 1915.

which became, in 1921, the Military Academy where—because of a policy of exclusion—only presidential guards and officers, who were all mulattoes, were accepted because they are part of the Haitian elite and the bourgeoisie.[272] Moreover, in 1923, a rural police force was formed, and it was composed of 551 deputies and section chiefs; they were trained to patrol and secure the remote areas.[273] In 1928, the forces were combined to be called the National Guard or "Guard of Haiti" to professionalize the institution by building police stations, prisons, customs, and fire stations.

In 1954, after the coup d'état from General Kebreau against the populist government of Daniel Fignole, the youth from La Saline[274] and Bel-Air[275]—grouped under the revolutionary theme *Rouleau Compresseur* (steamroller)—invaded the streets of the capital of Port-au-Prince with fire and blood. By attacking Fort Dimanche, a military bastion known as a place of torture and for its toughness against opponents, over five hundred young people have died under military fire. In September 1957, Francois "Papa Doc" Duvalier came to power; he wanted to keep it for the rest of his life while intending to transfer it to his son Jean-Claude "Baby Doc" Duvalier. To maintain his power, he appealed to Clement Barbot to create a loyal armed group called the Cagoulards, whose members come from the poorest areas of the country. Having not satisfied, Papa Doc wanted a repressive force that is better organized and involved in the daily life of every citizen. In fact, the Cagoulards, altogether with the heads of sections or the rural police force, were to be recycled into another paramilitary

---

[272] In 1929, statistics show that less than 40 percent of army officers are Haitians.

[273] Martin-Luc, BONNARDOT and Gilles DANROC, "The fall of the Duvalier house: Texts for history," Montreal, KARTHALA Editions, 1989, p. 124.

[274] Popular district on the outskirts of Port-au-Prince.

[275] *Id.*

group whose members are notoriously known as the Tonton Macoutes. Lacking confidence in the new Haitian army, created by the United States and now officially called the Armed Forces of Haiti (AFH), which had a workforce of five thousand soldiers, Papa Doc had increased the size of its paramilitary force, totaling twenty-five thousand members. The Tonton Macoutes would counterbalance the weight of the army, which was considered by many as a professional and traditional force in the destabilization of civil governments. This was to provide also a black militia to deal with the mulatto power.[276] In late 1959, the Tonton Macoutes had recognizable equipment: dark glasses, dressed in blue jeans, and armed with old rifles and machetes. They were known everywhere as the government's *Civil Militia*. Aside from their counterbalance power, their main mission was to play the role of informants and detect conspiracies, such as invasions of Fort Liberte and Ouanaminthe by General Cantave in September 1963.[277] Whereas, two years earlier, Papa Doc closed the doors of the Military Academy; and, in 1964, after the death of Clement Barbot, he renamed the militia under the official name of Volontaires de la Sécurité Nationale (VSN), whose members were already under direct presidential control. Young men and women from poor neighborhoods and rural areas were recruited and integrated into the militia. A branch of the VSN body, created just for women, called Fillettes Laleau, is led by Rosalie Bousquet—who was notoriously known as Madame Max Adolph—the terrible commander of Fort Dimanche and, later, the chief of the militia. Unlike the traditional recruitment of girls in Africa, these "recruits" were not used as sexual objects and should not be submitted or having to cook for their male counterparts. However, they were armed to the teeth. They were unforgivable, and, often,

---

[276] M.-L. BONNARDOT and G. DANROC, *loc. cit.*, note 273, p. 124.

[277] General Cantave organized his invasion with his armed group of 210 men, including the popular child soldier Bernard Sansaricq, who is freshly graduated from the Bordentown Military Institute.

they were more dangerous than the men themselves. Girls and women who joined the group were generally more dedicated to serve because of their ambitions comparing to their opposite sex.[278]

With the death of the "President for Life" Francois "Papa Doc" Duvalier, in April 1971, and the accession of his son Jean-Claude "Baby Doc" Duvalier in power, the wind blows again to the army's side: men in green (soldiers) and men in blue (the police).[279] Other changes may be the creation of the Corps of Leopards, an anti-guerrilla force who has experienced a great defeat in January 1982 on the island of Tortuga during an invasion of the Kamoken—the armed group of Bernard Sansaricq, whose members were trained overseas.[280] The Haitian army, whose number is five thousand soldiers in 1957 and seven thousand soldiers in 1985, with a budget estimated at 25 percent of government spending, the Tonton Macoutes' power is now absolute with the official support of the army. The militia terrorized anywhere, anytime, and anyone; even members of the diplomatic corps, the army, and the clergy were not spared from this terror.

In fact, five years earlier, Mrs. Horace Coriolan—the Fillette Laleau's commander in the region of Kenscoff—used four girls, who were also his nieces and members of the militia, to attack the Afe Neg Koumbit grassroots organization, which was led by Father Occide Jeanty, also known as Pè Siko or Father Siko. Unfortunately, this Catholic priest became a few weeks later a powerful "leader macoute" for his own protection. Meanwhile, the members of the army were organized: on the one hand, the army or the "men in blue"—who

---

[278] Elizabeth ABBOTT, "Haiti: The Duvaliers and Their Legacy," New York, McGraw-Hill Book Company, 1988, 382 p. 87.

[279] Before 1971, the soldiers were all dressed in khaki.

[280] Bernard SANSARICQ, « Le pouvoir de la foi », Montréal, Éditions Du Marais, 2006, p. 104.

played the role of police—created the Detection Service, known for their cruelty as SD,[281] a form of intelligence service that works on behalf of the Duvalier dictatorship. The Service Detection became a few years later the Department of Criminal Investigations, which was later replaced by the Anti-Gang Service. On the other hand, the army or the "men in olive green" continued to forcibly recruit young farmers to become Tonton Macoutes to fight the Kamoken.

Meanwhile, different left-wing groups started to regroup in the recruitment of young people, students, and intellectuals. Political parties now have their own armed groups operating in the dark and use violence as a means of pressure.[282] But, on November 27, 1985, the army responded with violence in Gonaives to eliminate the insurgents[283] with the support of the Tonton Macoutes. The next day, three schoolboys[284] were killed by members of the militia. This monumental political blunder enabled the globalization of the armed struggle in different poor neighborhoods of the country: mobilization and the long-term institutionalization of the movement *déchoukage*[285] by popular organizations in Haiti. Indeed, young and old alike refused to go to school out of fear or willingness to mobilize themselves

---

[281] Political police who work in concert with the military, the police, and the militiamen and whose commander is Col. Albert Pierre, well known under the name of Ti-boulé.

[282] M.-L. BONNARDOT and G. DANROC, *loc. cit.*, note 273, p. 254.

[283] Jean-Pierre Baptiste, alias Jean Tatoune, was one of the insurgents and young leaders of the revolutionary and anti-Duvalier movement in Gonaïves. After going back to his old group in 1991, he took up for the military and the neo-Duvalierists; he became the local leader of the paramilitary group FRAPH. We saw him, in 1994, at the head of a battalion of ten soldiers in Raboteau. He was sentenced to hard labor for life for his participation in the massacre. He escaped from prison in August 2002; and, in January 2004, he gave his services to the Cannibal Army and swore to overthrow the government of Aristide.

[284] Jean-Robert Cius, Mackenson Michel, and Daniel Israel.

[285] Lynching of Tonton Macoutes and destruction of private property.

against the government. University students and members of unions called a general mobilization. Mafia organizations are formed, and politicians subsidized criminal groups. The proliferation of grassroots organizations is increasing every minute in the four corners of the country. New and young leaders of popular and grassroots organizations wanted to be heard in declaring their intention to take "emergency measures"[286] and radical actions against the government in power. Leaflets and graffiti are seen everywhere in the streets and walls of major cities of the country. In fact, in one of these leaflets published incognito and numbered by the members of the Opération Prends Garde, the opposition movement, it says, "We need young people to get justice, killers must be tried publicly . . . if delivery can not happen naturally, we are ready to do a cesarean. Down with repression, liberty or death!" And, a few days later, the Caesarean operation was launched!

On the eve of the fall of Jean-Claude Duvalier, the militia has a membership of three hundred thousand members, of whom forty thousand were well armed and equipped. On the day of Baby Doc's departure to exile, on February 6, 1986, the militia was attacked and routed following a popular uprising of young children and old people, men, and women. Many Tonton Macoutes were killed, burned alive,[287] or forced to flee. Children, like adults, invaded the streets in search of their victims while joyfully chanting in Creole, "Yon jou pou chasè, yon jou pou jibye!"[288] They quickly organized themselves as the Brigades of Vigilance[289] to consolidate their

---

[286] *Letter from the Youth of Artibonite*, La Crête-à-Pierrot, 6 January 1986.

[287] By "Father Lebrun," a form of torture called *Supplice du collier*. Activists put flaming tires in the neck of some individuals or their enemies while pouring gasoline to deliver the final blow to their victims.

[288] Yesterday it was the hunters; today, it's the hunted's turn!

[289] With a total membership of seven thousand members.

power. Each neighborhood had its own brigade, and that was the confusion: innocent people were killed, acts of reckoning, and mob justice in action. The army took revenge[290] during the November 1987 election by leaving voters at the mercy of the militiamen who did not care if their family members were there. They used their machine guns and their machetes on anyone who were waiting to vote at the Turgeau polling station. In September 1988, members of the Brassards Rouges—another paramilitary neo-Duvalierist—invaded the church of St. Jean Bosco, killed a score of followers, and set fire to the building while the Catholic priest Jean-Bertrand Aristide officiated the Mass. The same year, to counter the action of the wildly popular and grassroots organizations, another armed group known as the Zenglendo, whose members operate regularly during the night, attacked militants of the brigades. This paramilitary group, who was strongly associated with the Duvalier and neo-Duvalierist's regimes, was surely attacking with cruelty with the blessing of the Haitian army. And, in 1991, the attachés were acting even worse than the Zenglendo. As another paramilitary group, which serves the political purposes of the military and the police, their main purpose was to collect information about people's movements, to put under arrest (legally or illegally), and to eliminate the troublemakers.

5.2 *The armed actors in the conflict*

Under international law, a "civil war" is primarily a noninternational armed conflict taking place on the territory of a State, between the armed forces and dissident armed forces or organized armed groups that, under the leadership of a responsible official, exercise a part of its territory as it allows them to conduct

---

[290] Gen. Henry Namphy, also head of the National Council of Government (CNG), declared, "There is only one voter, the army!" Cf. E. ABBOTT, *op. cit.*, note 278, p. 358.

continued and concentrated military operations.[291] Thus, in regard to Haiti, there are many armed actors, and they are changing sides more or less every time there is political tension and a new government. These actors are the Haitian armed forces, the national police, international security forces, multinational forces for security and stability, and political parties, as well as armed groups that are anti and pro government. In fact, according to a well-known Haitian political analyst, "after the fall of Jean Claude Duvalier in 1986 the country became a labyrinth. From 1986 to 2006, they [the players] have embarked on a dangerous political adventure without considering the difficulties related to the transformation of social structures and economic policies"[292] of the country.

5.2.1   The Haitian armed forces and the
          international and multinational forces

The Haitian armed forces, as they were before the departure of Jean-Claude Duvalier, have not changed. With a workforce of seven thousand men, divided into branches of the military, police, the air corps, navy, or coast Guard, these forces resist change and stand firm to their old tradition of watchdogs. Nevertheless, we must admit that the Armed Forces of Haiti (FAD'H) are the only hierarchized organization that has the merit of being a proud, strong, and solid institution. It is the only institution that can secure the country in times of crisis, disorder, and chaos. However, the military could not play their catalytic role in stabilizing the country. They have missed their vocation from this wonderful opportunity that fate had presented them on a silver platter in the wake of February 1986, which is evidenced by the following multiple blunders: in April 1986, soldiers

---

[291] HIGH COMMISSIONER, *op. cit.*, note 19, p. 79. *Supra*, note 61.

[292] Jean E. RENÉ, "A lost country," Haiti Promotional Group for Democracy, 4 August 2006.

shot on the crowd under the command of Isidore Pognon, commander of Fort Dimanche; the laissez-faire of armed groups under the control of landowners in the region of Jean-Rabel in July 1987 when more than two hundred peasants who are members of the peasant association Tèt Ansamn were killed after being ambushed;[293] in November 1987, the illegal decommissioning of the members of the Provisional Electoral Council and the postponement of presidential elections; the overthrow of the elected president of Haiti, Leslie Manigat, in June 1988; torture of "All Saints Prisoners"[294] under Gen. Prosper Avril's order in 1989; a year later, the same general is involved in the case of "Piatre Massacre," where several farmers were killed.

Certainly, the most critical blunder is the bloody coup d'état of September 29, 1991, against Pres. Jean-Bertrand Aristide, who was elected freely in February 1991 with 67 percent of the vote. The armed forces should have left the constitutional order to take its course instead of forcing the populist priest to leave power. The army should have stayed put and played its role as a catalyst of changes without deeply involving itself into overthrowing nonpromilitary governments. Moreover, following his accession to the highest office of the state, speeches and the president's actions were no longer "Catholic" and would have caused sooner or later his downfall. By the deliberate violence seen in his speeches might well be considered as arrogant by many. Otherwise, for the military, those acts will bring ipso facto a new social politico-economical order that will engage deeply the Haitian society. By cutting short this democratic experience, this blunder has resulted, first, to the demobilization of the Armed Forces of Haiti (FAD'H); and, second, to the creation of a new police force under foreign tutelage. Also, it has contributed to the

---

[293] Called "the massacre of Jean-Rabel," July 27, 1987.

[294] Evans Paul, a.k.a. K-Plim, and Marino Étienne were arrested by the army during the Day of the Dead.

intervention—on Haitian ground—of international security forces[295] as well as other multinational forces that encompass security, peace, and stability.[296]

Indeed, with the return of President Aristide in October 1994 and the departure into exile of Gen. Raoul Cedras and other members of his staff, the army is weakened and is now under the mercy of a vengeful president.[297] A year after his return to power and with the assistance of the UN and other international partners, a new national police force is created with the demobilized soldiers. A few months later, those soldiers were not to be found in the new police force because they were booted out.[298] In fact, to control the armed groups, the UN asked the Aristide government that the status of armed security personnel who is not part of the National Police of Haiti (PNH) is to be regularized. For the UN, the regularization of these armed groups is important since the measure will force the leaders of these groups to be responsible for the activity of its members, especially when members are involved in crime or violations of human rights. Therefore, according to the UN, the country's civil courts have jurisdiction over the defendants and justice will grant no more impunity for these perpetrators who commit willful acts that are considered war crimes.[299]

With these new police force and the regularization of these pro-government armed groups, the Aristide government began to integrate its own "men" who have no training or education. Sure

---

[295] The armed forces of the United States and France.

[296] The multinational forces of the UN and the OAS.

[297] In 1995, President Aristide signed a decree demobilizing the army to protect himself.

[298] These soldiers were replaced by members of pro-government armed groups.

[299] AG Res. 1994/67, 9 March 1994.

enough, former members of vigilante groups became members of the new police force. Thus, the settling of old scores is beginning to be seen and political crimes are committed in broad daylight. One of the unsolved cases is a double murder in March 1995[300] and another double murder in August 1996.[301]

On the other hand, the international security forces and multinational forces security and stability want to help and comfort the Haitian problem following a specific request of Pres. Jean-Bertrand Aristide. Indeed, from exile in 1993, the Haitian president called on United Nations and the friends of Haiti to strengthen the embargo against the military junta, and in February 1993, the International Civilian Mission in Haiti (MICAH) arrived in Port-au-Prince with this triple mandate: providing technical assistance, providing support for the implementation of a program to promote and defend human rights, and monitoring compliance by Haiti of human rights and fundamental freedoms.

In agreement with the Governor's Island,[302] an American intervention force arrived in Haiti in September 1994 to secure the country before the return of exiled president. In March 1995,

---

[300] Mireille Durocher Bertin, lawyer and opponent of the government, and one of her clients, Eugène Baillergeau, were killed by machine guns bursting bullets.

[301] The Federal Bureau of Investigation (FBI), in its investigation report, assures that the murders of Pastor Antoine Leroy and Jacques Florival, two members of the Movement for National Development (MDN), were attributable to agents of the Presidential Security Office Unit (USP) of Pres. René Préval— the successor and "twin brother" of Pres. Jean-Bertrand Aristide. *See* Marcelle VICTOR, "Details on violence and assassinations: The Origins of Current Violence in Haiti," *Haiti Promotional Group for Democracy*, 3 August 2006.

[302] Signed in New York, on July 3, 1993, by the two parties to the conflict (Aristide and Cédras); one of the provisions of this agreement is the unconditional return to constitutional order.

the US military transferred control of the intervention force to the multinational forces of the United Nations Organization (UNO) and the Organization of American States (OAS). Both organizations have mandated the United Nations Mission in Haiti (UNMIH) to help implement certain provisions of the agreement, help modernize the Haitian armed forces and create a new police force, and hold parliamentary elections free and fair.[303]

In June 1996, the new Mission Support United Nations in Haiti (UNSMIH) is mandated to help the government improve the professional skills of police and maintain the security and stability.[304] In July 1997, to encourage the professionalization of the national police, the Transition Mission in Haiti United Nations (UNTMIH) is created at the behest of the Security Council.[305] In November 1997, a new mission has arrived, and this time, it's the Civilian Police Mission in United Nations in Haiti (MIPONUH), whose mandate is to assist the government in providing assistance to the professionalization of the police and to focus on advisory activities and training of specialized units.[306] In March 2000, the International Mission for Support in Haiti (MICAH) replaced MIPONUH to consolidate the results obtained by previous missions, to promote human rights and strengthen the institutional activity of the police

---

[303] CS Res. 867, 23 September 1993. In 1995, this mission had a staff of 6,055 soldiers and 847 police officers. In 1996, the strength was 1,200 military, 300 police, 160 international civilians, 180 local civilians, and 18 volunteers, with a total cost of $337 million.

[304] CS Res. 1063, 28 June 1996. Strength: 1,281 soldiers and 268 police officers. Cost: $60 million.

[305] CS Res. 1123, 30 July 1997. Staff: 250 police officers and 50 soldiers. Cost: $10 million.

[306] CS Res. 1141, 28 November 1997. Staff: 300 police officers, 72 international civilians, 133 local civilians and 17 volunteers. Cost: $20.4 million.

and the judiciary, and to coordinate the international community's dialogue with political and social actors.[307]

Despite the presence of all these missions in Haiti, nothing has changed, for, in November 2000, a political crisis over the results of parliamentary elections forced the opposition to boycott presidential elections in June 2001; launch of Operation Zero Tolerance[308] by the government under the pretext of fighting against crime and, in December 2001, reprisals against the opposition who is accused of orchestrating an attempted coup against the government in August 2002; launch of Operation Punch by the Cannibal Army to free their leader, Amiot Metayer, from prison in Gonaives and, in December 2002, summary execution of three Viola's son Robert to the police station by police Carrefour; and anti-government protests are increasing and increasing violence perpetrated by pro-government gangs.

In February 2004, "to spare Haiti a civil war," the Security Council voted unanimously to authorize the deployment of the Multinational Interim Force in Haiti (MIF) to "disarm 25,000 Haitians in possession of weapons."[309] According to many, this new multinational force failed in their mission because it is unable to guarantee public safety. Finally, in June 2004, the interim force is replaced by the United Nations Mission for Stabilization in Haiti (MINUSTAH), whose mandate is to assist the transitional government

---

[307] AG Res. 54/193, 17 December 1999. Staff: eighty technicians providing advice and material assistance to the police and the judiciary.

[308] This operation by the government of Aristide contributed to the emergence of these pro-government armed groups: Bale Wouze, Zéro Tolérance, Basen San, Pèdi Pa Chache, Zo Bouke Chen, 5th Column, Special Brigade, Palmantè Lanmò, Zobop, etc. See appendix (figure 6).

[309] CS Res. 1529, 29 February 2004. Strength: 3,600 American, French, Canadian and Chilean soldiers.

to ensure security and stability in the country and to bring support to the process of reforming the national police.[310]

5.2.2 The political parties and armed movements

Apart from the Haitian government forces and international and multinational forces, we must say that pro-government armed groups, political parties, and armed opposition groups play a major role in destabilizing politically the country. The armed conflict, a chronic problem, which involves the socioeconomic development of Haiti, cannot be ended if the various actors in the conflict manipulate the situation to their advantage or try to cling to their personal ambitions at the expense of an entire nation. Above all, being a leader of a political party, a public or private institution, and even an armed group requires exemplary behavior for the well-being of the community and the civic education of the young people. The leader must communicate his values and attitudes, his beliefs and behavior, his culture, his motivation and aspirations, and his norms and rules of conduct to contribute positively to the smooth running of the society in which he lives and he is responsible of.[311] Unfortunately, many of these actors do not have these positive qualities of leadership.

Although, during the reign of the Duvalier (father and son), people who were exercising their civil and political rights have been severely punished—because of their ideology and their political affiliation or membership[312]—we can say openly that the absence of organized crime, characterized by using these armed gangs to put pressure and fear in the streets under the acts of killing, raping, and kidnapping

---

[310] CS Res. 1542, 30 April 2004. Staff: 6,600 soldiers and 1,700 police officers. Brazil oversees this new mission.

[311] Allan D. ENGLISH, "Understanding Military Culture: A Canadian Perspective," Montreal, McGill-Queen's University Press, 2004, p. 21.

[312] Most academics and intellectuals during this period opted for communism.

in series, is enough so that people felt safe. The fall of the Duvalier régime and the advent of other social and political unrests after 1986 were mainly caused by charismatic figures like the Rev. Sylvio Claude,[313] leader of the Haitian Christian Democratic Party (PDCH), and Gregory Eugene, a lawyer, a law professor, and a constitutional leader of the Social Christian Party of Haiti (PSCH). Later, at the dawn of the popular uprising of February 6, 1986, Jean-Bertrand Aristide—a Catholic priest of the Church of St. John Bosco who preached liberation theology to the masses—has become the largest responsible for the institutionalized social tear. Indeed, according to many, "this guy succeeds in transforming the dreams of democracy raised in 1986 by the fall of Baby Doc (Jean-Claude Duvalier) in an endless nightmare" for the people.[314]

Unlike other leaders, the speech of Jean-Bertrand Aristide is "both controversial and violent. First, it is controversial because the speaker does not explain what it is. Second, it is violent because of direct appeals to the people"[315] by inciting them to act in a violent manner. In fact, following February 6, 1986, the priest encouraged his young followers to kill, saying in verse 55 of his book of poems published in Creole, "Jistis balans, balans dechoukaj."[316] Entrenched in Cité

---

[313] Assassinated by an armed group in the locality of Léogâne, a town south of Port-au-Prince, during the military coup of September 29, 1991. According to the daughter of the political leader, the murder was committed under the instigation of Jean Claude Jean-Baptiste, who became *ad interim* director of the police force under Aristide's government.

[314] Jean-Michel DJIAN, « La grande désespérance », Jeune Afrique, No. 2452, 6-12 janvier 2008, p. 58.

[315] Creole words like *bayo sa yo merite* (give them what they deserve). *Cf.* Théodore ACHILLE, "Aristide: le dire et le faire," Montreal, Les Éditions de la Vérité, 1998, p. 55.

[316] Means the scale of justice is the scale of uprooting. *Cf.* Jean-Bertrand ARISTIDE, « 100 Vèsè Dechoukaj: Va t-en Satan », Pòtoprins, 7 fevrye 1986.

Soleil,[317] where he has followers who swear to remain faithful to him until death, Aristide took the opportunity to both exploit and help young, poor orphans of his orphanage La Fanmi Se Lavi. The priest has a personal vision of the future, but, above all, he should be elected president. Following the manipulation of his followers and because of his anti-macoutes and anti-imperialists writings, he was propelled into the national political scene, which allowed him to be chosen in place of Victor Benoît [318] as the primary candidate who can, with equal strengths, face up the anti-change forces under the banner of the National Front for Change and Democracy (FNCD).

Thus, on February 6, 1991, Jean-Bertrand Aristide became president of Haiti after winning the presidential election with most votes. After a coup undertaken by the armed forces on September 29, 1991, Aristide went into exile. In October 1994, returning from exile under the pressure of his followers in Haiti and abroad, with the support of the international community and under heavy military escort[319] and protection[320] of the United States of America, Aristide returned to the National Palace stronger than ever. According to some, he is no longer an innocent man; he became now a true chimère.[321] This characterization fits him well when his goal now is to rely more on the mass who is illiterate, the university students, and those poor slums to consolidate his power at all costs.

---

[317] The largest slum in the country with a population of three hundred thousand. See figures 3.2 and 3.3.

[318] Former leader of the National Committee of the Congress of Democratic Movements (KONAKOM), one of the former leaders of the Democratic Convergence, and, now, leader of the Fusion.

[319] Under the name of Operation Uphold Democracy.

[320] See appendix (figure 4).

[321] Term used to designate a member of pro-government armed groups as a murderer, bandit, or outlaw.

Indeed, the recruitment, the use, and the direct involvement of Haitian children in armed conflicts have never had such a large scale only after the return of President Aristide to power. Note that prior to his return, the children were not armed.[322] However, they have been used indirectly in armed conflict specifically in actions of civil disobedience and criminal—for example, in popular demonstrations such as setting flaming barricades, blocking streets, burning tires, threatening citizens by crushing their car windshields, undertaking déchoukage,[323] necklacing Macoutes,[324] and clubbing opponents.[325] But, since 1995, we see in Haiti[326] a direct participation of youth in armed conflicts, and it is also the beginning of a massive and unconditional high-powered arm race.

Note also that since the "return to constitutional order," we have seen some very young children become professional killers and members of death squads of pro-governmental armed gangs who are killing the members of the opposition.[327] For example, according to

---

[322] Except for those who were used in popular uprisings against the slave system (1702–1802), in the war of independence against France (1802–1804), in conflicts between armed groups, and against the American occupation (1806–1920). However, from 1920 until 1994, the enlistment, use, and direct involvement of children in armed conflict did not exist. After the return of Pres. Jean-Bertrand Aristide, those who are armed (street children and orphans) are recognized by the Haitian authorities as very dangerous elements called Kokorat and Ratpakaka, because of their age, their socioeconomic position, and their ease of following orders. These children are the first to be recruited to become real Chimères.

[323] *Supra*, note 285.

[324] *Supra*, note 287.

[325] *Supra*, note 301 (See Marcelle VICTOR).

[326] A/62/609-S/2007/757. According to the Security Council's "Shame List," Haiti is among eighteen countries in which children are recruited and involved in armed conflict.

[327] A fact very contradictory to the return to constitutional order. Indeed, according to article 268 of the Haitian Constitution of 1987, "military service is compulsory for all Haitians aged at least eighteen years; and, only the law

the testimony of a police officer, four street children had a mission to assassinate a member of the 184 Group—an organization of the opposition—and they will pretend to wipe his car windshields to carry out their criminal plan.[328] Many of these children are trained in handling weapons and in assassination techniques.

In fact, in 1995, the government appealed to "international experts" in Latin America to teach a first group of young old and new residents of the orphanage Lafanmi Se Lavi the techniques of political killings, while the techniques of weapons handling and other military issues are taught by "experts" in Haiti.[329] And, in a second group, it is the turn of young people who are also affiliated members of the Lavalas movement[330] who live in different neighborhoods and slums of the country. A few weeks later, they distributed weapons to all teenagers who took part in military training so they can be ready to defend their government at all costs.[331]

Moreover, politically serious divisions have emerged within the Lavalas movement, a movement that is initiated by President Aristide since his first term. These divisions, caused by the refusal of the president to share power, have enabled the Organisation

---

fixes the mode of recruitment, the duration and the operating rules of these services." Only one constitution that has allowed the recruitment of children under the age of eighteen, which is the Constitution of 1795, which, in article 277, recognizes that "all citizens and sons of citizens able to bear arms" must be part of the sedentary national guard (the reserve army), while in the active army, the enrollments are done voluntarily (article 286).

[328] *Statement by police officer Jules Bélimaire*, Agent 3, 8 January 2004.

[329] *Supra*, note 301 (See Marcelle VICTOR).

[330] Creole word for "flood": according to this movement, fanatics will have to destroy everything they find in their path, including people who are not Lavalas and as well as properties that do not belong to Lavalas.

[331] Miguelito, "Haiti 2006: Little Recent History of Armed Bands (Gangs)," 2 June 2006.

Politique Lavalas (OPL) to change its name to Organization of People in Struggle (OPL), whereas from the president's own plan, he took the initiative to create and run his new political party called the Lavalas Family. It is important to note that the split was caused by disagreements about economic policy and by the outcome of the senatorial elections of April 1997 during the presidency of René Préval. As it has often been said, friends of yesterday become today's enemies. The struggle between these two groups that were once united under the same political banner of the National Front for Change and Democracy (FNCD) has allowed the former Tonton Macoutes, the demobilized soldiers, as well as the paramilitary neo-Duvalierists and the pro-governmental armed groups to turn to the opposition for restructuration while they are happily watching the sad spectacles of internal political struggle for their moment of glory to arrive.

If the Haitian government forces (the army and the police) were the only constitutionally recognized organizations to have a monopoly on security and violence,[332] other forces are already beginning to mobilize. Determined to return to action, these former members of the VSN corps,[333] as well as the attachés (undercover agents) and former soldiers who have been unemployed, have formed a paramilitary group called FRAPH (Armed Revolutionary Front for Haitian Progress). The group, led by Emmanuel "Toto" Constant[334]

---

[332] Title XI, articles 264 and 269 of the *Haitian Constitution*, ratified on March 29, 1987.

[333] The National Security Volunteers (VSN) were demobilized by the National Council of Government (CNG) upon the departure of Jean-Claude "Baby Doc" Duvalier in February 1986.

[334] The New York Federal Court believes that Constant—a contract employee of the Central Intelligence Agency (CIA)—is responsible for crimes of torture and crimes against humanity in favor of several women who survived those acts, which were attributed to FRAPH. In October 2006, the court ordered him to pay $19 million in damages. And, in January 2008, he refused to plead

and Louis-Jodel Chamblain,[335] decided to act and strike savagely the Lavalas Family members and the supporters of the Lavalas government with their well-known Death Squad wing. As a prelude to their armed movement, in October 1993, this paramilitary group took up arms and, with false nationalistic sentiments, started chanting revolutionary and anti-American slogans as if they are ready to fight if there is a military invasion. With the support of the Haitian armed forces, they undertook different mass media campaigns against the Lavalas grassroots movement; they organized events on the wharf in Port-au-Prince against the ultimate return of President Aristide particularly when the *Harlan County*[336] has reached the harbor. In April 1994, soldiers of the Haitian armed forces and the paramilitary group FRAPH jointly undertook a series of attacks against the slum of Raboteau before investing it by force. During that single day, it was estimated there were between twenty and fifty people have been killed either by bullets or under the blows of machetes and many Lavalas Family members and supporters were drowned while attempting to flee by sea.[337]

Finally, suspicions that are arisen against the Lavalas Family government over the death of Jean Dominique and Brignol Lindor (two well-known journalists) and the death of Amiot "Cuban"

---

guilty to real estate fraud in the Brooklyn Supreme Court.

[335] Member of the army and leader of several paramilitary groups from the elections of November 1987 until the overthrow of the government of Jean-Bertrand Aristide in February 2004. Accused of intentional homicide, he surrendered himself to justice after an arrest warrant issued by the transitional government of Gérard Latortue; then he was released after a few months in prison.

[336] First ship of an American security force preparing for Aristide's return.

[337] AMNESTY INTERNATIONAL, "HAITI: Justice is still awaited," July 1, 1998.

Metayer, leader of the Cannibal Army in Gonaives,[338] have worsened the political situation in Haiti. On the one hand, a demonstration of the Group of 184, which was heading toward the main square in Port-au-Prince, has been disrupted by a crowd of supporters and members of Lavalas Family that have surrounded the march and started throwing stones and bottles on those who were marching. On the other hand, state officials and activists from the Lavalas Family political movement has been targeted by a group of gunmen from the Armée Sans Manman,[339] an armed gang from the commune of Belladère. There is also the involvement of members of the Haitian police force as well as those who are close to the government in drug trafficking, which is controlled largely by the Colombian cartels.[340]

In December 2003, several sectors of the Haitian society (students, trade unionists, and businessmen of the 184 Group) launched their peaceful movement called Grenn Nan Bouda (GNB)[341] to force the government to resign. As part of this movement, a conflict erupted in the city of Gonaives in early February 2004 and then quickly spread to other parts of the country. In the ranks of the insurgents are mostly

---

[338] See appendix (figure 6).

[339] A new armed group composed in part of former Haitian army soldiers.

[340] The American justice system, through the American federal agency—the Drug Enforcement Administration (DEA)—and the federal courts have found these Haitian authorities guilty for drug trafficking: Evens Brillant (former head of the Bureau de Lutte Contre le Drug Trafficking), Fourel Célestin (former president of the Haitian Senate), Elnu Moise (former national police officer), Oriel Jean (former security chief of the National Palace), etc.

[341] Creole word that means "someone who has balls" or "courageous." Aristide's government reacted violently against this movement by using his supporters and members of his armed groups, with the help of the police, against students who demonstrated in the grounds of the State University of Haiti (UEH), where more than twenty people, mainly students, were reportedly injured. However, Pierre-Marie Paquiot, the university president, was beaten with an iron bar and had both legs broken, while the vice president of the university—Wilson Laleau—miraculously emerged with an injury on his head.

demobilized soldiers, including former leaders of the Armed Forces of Haiti (FAD'H), members of the Armed Revolutionary Front for Haitian Progress (FRAPH), and members of the Cannibal Army,[342] a pro-governmental armed group, which has decided for now to switch to the opposition. Several days of fighting ensued, and over 70 percent of large cities have fallen under the control of insurgents.[343] Thus, very early on February 29, 2004, while the rebels threatened to march on Port-au-Prince and to violently take the National Palace, President Aristide left the country—a moment of glory that will be only short term for some of these insurgents who have very shaky backgrounds.[344]

---

[342] The leader of the group, Amiot Métayer, is assassinated under the orders of President Aristide, who is afraid of seeing him supporting the opposition, for the government depends heavily on this group for control of Gonaïves and the entire Central Plateau region—key places where the greatest Haitian revolutionaries were born. After Amiot's death, his brother Butteau took over the leadership of the group and sided with anti-government forces to avenge his brother.

[343] The rebels are led by Guy Philippe, ex-commissioner of the Haitian National Police, and Louis-Jodel Chamblain, former commander of FRAPH.

[344] *Supra*, note 334 (See also note 335).

CHAPTER 6

The Recent Evolution of
the Armed Conflict

The political impasse that is blocking the country for several years, the national economy that depends on foreign aid and the Haitian diaspora, the systemic impunity that is deeply rooted in the Haitian justice system, which is offered to the highest bidder, the scourge of drugs dealings, and the rise of armed groups are forcing the country to become ultimately "the theater of acts of violence, apparently in criminal nature, but whose origin is difficult to determine; some directly hit opponents of the government, while others appear to deliberately target government and police officials."[345] Thus, promoting a political approach in the regulation of disputes or noninternational armed conflicts[346] that require rather a legal approach under international standards and regulations that have been ratified, the international community—through its international bodies establishing international missions for stability, peace, and security—is likely to provide conflicting solutions to the problem of child soldiers in Haiti.

6.1 Narco-trafficking, armed groups, and conflict

According to Amnesty International, the actions of armed criminal gangs who are often involved in drug trafficking or other

---

[345] *Supra*, note 337.

[346] N. ARZOUMANIAN and F. PIZZUTELLI, *loc. cit.*, note 3, p. 847. *Supra*, note 26.

forms of smuggling are a major problem for the new police force that lacks experience, and some members, moreover, have sometimes been tempted to involve themselves in such illicit activities. Amnesty International also believes that some of these gangs are handled by former members of the Haitian armed forces, which is today dismantled, or by paramilitary groups who collaborated with them and sought thereby to destabilize the government. In addition to these problems are the "gangs are linked with mafia and those sectors of the drugs which proved to be very successful, and the kidnapping industry has moved to a different level: now the flood of dollars went in Cité Soleil and in the populous districts of the lower town where some believe the kidnapping revenue reaches more than a million U.S. dollars per month."[347]

Indeed, the dangerous links between drugs, armed groups, and internal conflict have been prepared carefully and strategically by the government on two levels. First, at the national police, according to Roland Boutin:[348] "Recruiting standards becoming less and less respected. There were at the National Police Academy many cadets who have, as their sole criterion, loyalty to the party in power."[349] He continues to say that many of these cadets are former members of the Lavalas movement; they are working in collusion with armed groups, and they are also controlled by the Colombian cartels and by the members of the Haitian government. In fact, several former police officers, top government officials, friends of the president, and members of the Haitian parliament are currently behind bars in the

---

[347] Nancy ROC, "Haiti: Insecurity and Its Dangerous Connections," AlterPresse, 23 August 2006.

[348] Former technical advisor to the National Police of Haiti from 1999 to 2001.

[349] Roland BOUTIN, "Haiti—The police state of Aristide," Le Devoir, 28-29 février 2004.

United States.[350] Second, at the level of armed groups, according to President Aristide himself: "The young, even *Lafanmi Selavi* children, did not think about the danger . . . they were always exposed to the danger of death, they were immune from the seeds of death by exposing themselves so they could obey those they love."[351] And by using these children as soldiers, "contrary to President Francois Duvalier who had created a hierarchical militia, Aristide had a complex and anarchic structure: he was the only leader and each Chimère[352] leader was all powerful in his own neighborhood, but none of them had authority over the others."[353]

Thus, after the departure of President Aristide, there was a political vacuum that many armed groups have exploited. Indeed, the heads of the Chimère who live in the various slums of the country, former members of the National Police, the Security Unit and the National Palace Guards (USGPN), and members of pro-government armed groups such as the Rats Army and those of Ti Bwa communities, Gran Ravin, and Nan Beni, have set up the Baghdad Operation to terrorize Port-au-Prince for months not only to force the return of their leader in power but also to have funds to finance their

---

[350] *Supra*, note 340.

[351] Jean-Bertrand ARISTIDE, "Theology and Politics," Montreal, Les Éditions du CIDIHCA, 1995, p. 51.

[352] New pro-government armed group bringing together former affiliated members of the Lavalas movement, former residents of the Lafanmi Selavi orphanage and young people living in slums. This armed group, after the departure of President Aristide, undertook Operation Baghdad I and II to force his return from exile through theft, rape, kidnapping, and murder of ordinary citizens. See figure 6.

[353] *Supra*, note 329. *Cf.* Cité Soleil has thirty-two districts. Each district has a base. The bases were created as support groups for Aristide, a continuation of the Comités de Quartiers, which appeared shortly after the fall of Jean-Claude Duvalier.

movement while protecting the flow of cocaine.[354] While the political void is growing, the mafia organizations are developing their strategies to triple the drug trade in four years.[355] Therefore, young Chimère leaders such as Billy, 2Pac,[356] Evans-Ti Kouto, Amaral Duclona, Belony, Dread Wilmer, and Ti Bazil are armed with their AK-47 to defend their government at any cost.[357]

6.2 Intensification and internationalization

If the interim government would take office immediately after the departure of President Aristide, members of the Security Council have themselves authorized on the same day the deployment of a Multinational Interim Force in Haiti (MIFH) for a period of three months. Soldiers of the US Marines as well as soldiers from the French Army have landed.[358] Shortly after the departure of the marines and the arrival of the Brazilian force who will lead the mission of stability, the Baghdad Operation began.[359]

---

[354] The Baghdad Operation in Haiti is a copycat of the terrorist movements in Iraq that operate through kidnapping for ransom, rape, murder, and torture of civilians who are taken prisoner; the police have their heads decapitated. *Cf.* The Inter-American Commission on Human Rights (CIDH), referring to a report by the Justice and Peace Commission (CJP) of the Haitian Catholic Church, estimates that 2,015 people have died of violent deaths in Port-au-Prince during the last three years, of which only 1,151 between March 2004 and June 2005.

[355] Christophe WARGNY, "Political anarchy, Freezing of international aid. In Haiti, drugs as a substitute for development," Le Monde Diplomatique, June 2001, p. 20.

[356] *Supra*, note 352. 2Pac and Billy, child soldiers under the order of ex-president Aristide, are two brothers who both became lovers of Lélé, a French woman working for MICIVIH. *See* documentary: Asger LETH, "The Ghosts of Cité Soleil," Danish Film Institute, 2005.

[357] Joe MOZINGO, "Film links Aristide to Warlords," *Miami Herald,* 20 March 2006.

[358] See appendix (figures 3, 4 and 5).

[359] Madeline MACADONALO, "Haiti-U.N. Violence: These bastards of

In fact, since February 2004, politically motivated violence has reached unprecedented heights in Haiti. The cycle of terror triggered "by radical supporters of Jean-Bertrand Aristide has peaked in the summer of 2005 by a wave of kidnappings for ransom and targeted attacks."[360] In fact, if the international community has lent its support to the Haitian problem through its international and multinational forces for peace, security, and stability, it is because Haiti—since October 24, 1945—is part of this community with its rights as a full voting member. Haiti has signed the Universal Declaration of Human Rights in 1948, one of the international documents that inspired Haitians legislators to draft the new Constitution of 1987. Haiti has ratified the Convention on the Prevention and Punishment of the Crime of Genocide in 1950 and the International Covenant on Civil and Political Rights in 1991, but it has not ratified the Covenant on Economic, Social, and Cultural Rights as well the Convention against Torture and Other Cruel, Inhuman or Degrading.

In term of rights for children, although Haiti has ratified the Convention on the Rights of the Child in 1990, it has not ratified the protocol that protects children against their recruitment and involvement in armed conflict. Worse, Haiti is not even interested in the Convention on the Worst Forms of Child Labor, which is, according to many, an important matter for the future of Haitian children when 80 percent of the rural population live below the poverty threshold and that over 50 percent of the population are under eighteen years of age. Despite these ratifications,[361] it looks like Haiti is far from having an adequate legal system that can help promote

---

MICIVIH," Haiti Promotional Group for Democracy, 22 August 2006. *Supra*, note 352 (See also note 354).

[360] Radio Kiskeya, 8 June 2006.

[361] See appendix (figure 5).

justice when it ignores other conventions that are part of the core of international humanitarian law and international law of human rights.

The intensification of the armed conflict and the internationalization of the plight of Haiti are justified by the refusal of actors in conflict to promote the different international instruments Haiti has ratified; to cooperate between themselves in protecting the Haitian soil against foreign protectorate; to understand the danger the country faces; to put aside their personal ambitions at the expense of the nation; and to work together to bring Haiti back on a new democratic road, but sure. Do not forget also, according to many, that the international community bears the greatest burden of this crisis. In fact, after only five years in working to support the fledgling national police, the United Nations (UN) withdrew its forces. It is as if, for some, "they throw the police officers into the lion's mouth and making them indebted and dependent on the political power, which extends its claws on the national, regional and local fronts."[362]

6.3 The political approach of the UN without any regard for a legal solution

The withdrawal of the United Nations (UN) troops in Haiti, in 2000, caused a greater political instability. The international community, though imbued with the manipulation of the Aristide government to control the national police, continues to train and equip the armed group members, supporters, and government sympathizers who are integrated into the national police. Already, numerous meetings with senior leaders of the national police and government officials have convinced some members of the multinational force to stop the project.[363] Instead of ending the

---

[362] *Supra*, note 349.

[363] *Id.*

existence of the state police, numerous cases of corruption, breaches of law, and the nonrespect for human rights, the international community calls for dialogue and negotiations to resolve the crisis. And, according to Roland Boutin, this same international community has invested so much money and effort in a protracted crisis "without understanding" the Aristide Machiavellian program.[364] If for some, as is the case of Mr. Boutin, the international community has understood nothing of the Aristide project, for us, we can argue that they are very complicit. In fact, during the military coup of 1991, the International Civilian Mission in Haiti (MICAH) was primarily responsible for protecting the Lavalas militants who were persecuted by the Haitian military and paramilitary members of the Armed Revolutionary Front for Haitian Progress (FRAPH).

However, during this same period—according to many— "employees of this mission reinforced their links with the Lavalas leaders at the local, municipal, departmental and national levels."[365] For sure, many employees of the multinational force were recycled into the new force of the United Nations Mission for Stabilization in Haiti (MINUSTAH), which often acts in a partisan form: "The international community, the MINUSTAH, maintains a rather ambivalent attitude on this issue [of insecurity] by giving the impression that a situation of low-intensity violence is acceptable. The dangerous liaisons between the power of Lafanmi, the UN forces and gangs have realized the UN paradox in Haiti in this case, the same international forces that have invaded the country to rescue them from the dictatorship of Aristide in 2004, have helped bring and legitimatize that same power."[366]

---

[364] *Id.*

[365] *Supra,* note 359.

[366] *Supra,* note 347.

Indeed, during the February 7, 2006, presidential elections, supporters and sympathizers of President Aristide want to vote unanimously for René Préval,[367] a former prime minister under Aristide's government in 1991. By voting for him, the supporters of the ousted government want to accomplish two objectives: one, give back the power to a Lavalas member to return Aristide from exile; and, two, manipulate the government for control of all administrative offices. By contrast, Preval had only 48 percent of the popular votes, and—according to article 56 of the 1995 Electoral Law—he should get 50 percent plus one of the popular votes to win the presidential elections in the first round. Faced with a possibility of going to a second round, thousands of people (supporters and sympathizers of the deposed government), under the manipulation of Lavalas leaders, took to the streets demanding an immediate result.

The international community, particularly Latin American countries that are members of the multinational force, met secretly in the Mexican embassy in Port-au-Prince to find a "best solution" to this electoral crisis. Faced with a threatening mass that is becoming increasingly violent,[368] members of the international community— together with the interim government of Gerard Latortue[369]—forced members of the Provisional Electoral Council (CEP) to declare Rene Preval the president of Haiti without him going in the second round. In fact, the Organization of American States (OAS) had directly asked

---

[367] On December 17, 1995, the former prime minister René Préval was elected president of Haiti with more than 88 percent of the votes. During his first presidency, he was considered a puppet of Aristide. He even manipulated the legislative elections of May 2000 and led to the collapse of the Haitian parliament in favor of the return of President Aristide to power in February 2001.

[368] "Haiti: Protesters Reach Hotel Montana, UN Helicopters Fly Over Area," Haiti Press Network, February 13, 2006.

[369] See appendix (figures 4 and 5).

the CEP to count invalid ballots: a request that is in flagrant violation of the 1987 Haitian Constitution[370] and the Electoral Act of 1995.[371]

6.4 The DDR programs and the vigilante groups

Haiti has always been the scene of civil wars, armed struggles, and popular uprisings against the established political system. Since December 1492, political crimes that reach their highest and purest level are state violence that is always justified by a legal order.[372] In fact, in regard to Haiti's history, political crimes are a preventive action against threatening groups.[373] These groups, whose only objective is to overthrow the status quo on behalf of the people and then do nothing else to improve their situation, use the banditry and violence that are both closely linked to the proliferation of weapons. The lack of adequate measures for complete disarmament and an effective control of the flow of arms to Haiti has perpetuated and exacerbated the violence. The involvement of foreign countries in destabilizing Haitian politics is another major obstacle in controlling this proliferation.

Indeed, during the colonial era, the French armed the slaves against the Spaniards, who, in turn, did the same against the French. The British and Americans were arming the guerrilla in Ayiti against the French colonial order so they could enjoy many commercial

---

[370] Article 191 stipulates that "the Electoral Council is responsible for organizing and controlling in complete independence, all electoral operations throughout the territory of the Republic until the proclamation of the ballot."

[371] Article 109 stipulates that "the ballots on which the president [of the CEP] cannot recognize the intention or the political will of the voter are void. However, the votes cast in blank will be checked and counted."

[372] André CORTEN, "Demonization and Political Evil. Haiti: Misery, Religion, and Politics," Montreal, Les Éditions du CIDHICA-KARTHALA, 2000, p. 137.

[373] Id.

benefits.[374] The weapons proliferation does not stop after the Haitian independence because of the rich merchants, coming from different nationalities and backgrounds (Danish, Portuguese, Germans, and others), who continue to finance armed insurgencies against the government in power or other armed groups. However, throughout the history of the country, there are several attempts by established authorities who want to either stop or reduce this flow of arms. In this case, there were, during the last two centuries, at least five periods where several key Disarmament, Demobilization, and Reintegration (DDR) have occurred but did not reach their ultimate goal despite the dedication of the authorities.

6.4.1   The revolutionary period

During the revolutionary period, Thomas-François Galbaud[375] arrived on the island of Saint Domingue on June 20, 1793, and proclaimed himself governor. His main purpose was to prevent Sonthonax and Polverel,[376] two Jacobins commissioners, to achieve their anti-slavery goal, which would place whites, free blacks, and mulattoes on the same level of political equality. The next day, Galbaud conquered Cape after a furious battle against the republican forces of Sonthonax. After this defeat, not having enough fighters, the commissioners promised the slaves freedom if they agreed to help repel definitely the loyalist forces. Thus, on June 23, 1793, Macaya—a warlord—accepted the terms and brought with him his armed group of three thousand child soldiers. Pierrot, another warlord, also brought

---

[374] Pamphile D. LACROIX, *The Revolution of Haiti*, t.1 and 2, "Memories to serve in the history of the revolution of Saint-Domingue," 2nd ed. by P. Pluchon, Paris, Éditions KARTHALA, 1995, p. 357.

[375] French general and Napoleon's emissary, Galbaud was leading 1,200 sailors and 800 loyalist exiles aboard the warship *Jupiter 74* to fight the Jacobins.

[376] The two commissioners have with them only two hundred infantry soldiers and four hundred young mulatto combatants.

with him thousands of adults and child soldiers to invade the Cape with Macaya while forcing Galbaud to retreat and flee to France. Sonthonax and Polverel, hidden in the Breda area, returned to Cape after the battle and armed young black fighters with muskets they brought from France. Sonthonax, pointing to the muskets, exclaimed, "Behold your freedom! If you want to keep it, make good use of these rifles the day when whites will tell you to return them. For, he who will take away this gun will want you to be slaves!"

These words from Sonthonax still continue to resonate as a form of prophecy in the head of the Haitian fighters of all ages. In fact, the only idea of handing the weapons back to the authorities is, for many, the loss of their freedom and their ipso facto return to slavery. Indeed, Gen. Napoleon Bonaparte—with his secret agenda to restore slavery on the island—sent to Saint Domingue Gabriel Hedouville, as the new commissioner of the island, to disarm the black insurrectionists. On October 22, 1798, Toussaint Louverture is leading his armed group of twenty thousand Congos to counterattack and chase Hedouville, who quickly embarked for France with 1,800 refugees. After the arrest and the deportation of Toussaint, in June 1802, General Leclerc[377]—who is now the new master of the island—would not dare to undertake immediately a disarmament campaign. His main strategy is mainly to neglect the organization of the colonial army while organizing a new political and judicial system. A few weeks later, the general decided to integrate a third of the colonial army in the new gendarmerie. According to many, although the general has a willingness to disarm the black insurrectionists and to place the colony under the control of the French federation, the Disarmament, Demobilization, and Reintegration (DDR) program of 1802 would be long, risky, and

---

[377] Bonaparte's brother-in-law, Charles Leclerc, is general-in-chief of a new expedition of thirty thousand men to reestablish slavery in Saint-Domingue, where he died in November 1802 from yellow fever.

imperfect because of these four reasons. First, the inability to control, with a small number of troops, all the land of the colony. Second, the authorities could not recover all the weapons except for a total of thirty thousand rifles, while there were hundreds of weapons that were purchased by Toussaint from the English, Danes, and Americans were still missing. Third, the French authorities are beginning to multiply the executions of all those, while not considering age and sex, who get caught with weapons in hand. Finally, there were more than five hundred thousand individuals who were ever more determined not to suffer again the law of slavery.[378]

The 1802 DDR program, although the colonial authorities have decided to permanently suspend it, has caused, first, a popular discontent that is developed within a few days in several armed insurgencies. The latter were ultimately turned into a general uprising that will end on January 1, 1804, to Haitian independence. By contrast, these weapons—which were once used against the French, Spanish, and English—are turned now toward the Haitians themselves in internal conflicts that have lasted over a century. These fratricidal wars did stop upon the arrival of the marines on Haitian soil.

6.4.2   The American occupation period

During the occupation period, from 1915 to 1934, these weapons have found new targets: the Americans and their collaborators. In fact, sons and grandsons of the Independence War veterans, many of whom are also veterans of multiple civil wars that have devastated Haiti, the Cacos are both landless peasants and *Grandon* (farm owners) who are often used by politicians to overthrow governments in complete anarchy. Considered to be the most hard-core Haitian nationalists, they decide—through the techniques of guerrilla warfare—to fight a

---

[378] P. D. LACROIX, *op. cit.*, note 374, p. 357.

merciless war against the marines by undertaking several insurgency movements. Knowing that members of this armed group are particularly in the central and northern parts of the country, Col. Eli Cole—the commander of the First Marine Regiment—has established a DDR program that is focused only on the Cape and nearby cities to pacify and secure the region. His program is simple and contains two components: demobilize those who want to be paid[379] and punish those who refuse. Although powerful leaders of the Cacos want to be paid well to lay down arms and stop the rebellion,[380] the program is a failure. However, following the demobilization of the Haitian army during the first two years of the occupation, many ex-Cacos are reintegrated into the new state security force, such as the police, while their former leaders end up being either killed, executed, or murdered one after another.[381]

If the death of Benoît Batraville,[382] the last Cacos leader, ended the popular uprisings against the marines, it must be said that members of the rebel group and other members of society remain alert, and no authority would dare undertake overnight another DDR without any negative consequences. Certainly, everyone still remembers the words of Sonthonax and the disastrous consequences for the French federation. Moreover, armed conflicts continue to be funded by the same foreign traders and guided by new political actors and armed

---

[379] One hundred gourds for a Caco chief with his weapon and fifteen gourds for a Caco soldier with his weapon.

[380] Charles Zamor, brother of future Haitian president Oreste Zamor, wants to be paid $200,000 in gold.

[381] On October 31, 1919, betrayed by Jean-Baptiste Conzé for $3,000, Charlemagne Péralte was assassinated after being shot twice in the heart by Second Lieutenant Herman Hanneken, an American marine.

[382] On May 19, 1920, Benoît Batraville was hunted down and executed by a combined platoon of American marines and members of the Haitian gendarmerie.

groups. Once the gendarmerie is replaced by the Armed Forces of Haiti (FAD'H), true control instruments for the flow of arms and dreadful tools of repression against some paramilitary groups, a false sense of peace and security is established among Haitian citizens. But for how long?

6.4.3   The period of "constitutional return" to order

The third period in the Disarmament, Demobilization, and Reintegration (DDR) program in the history of Haiti coincides with the "return to constitutional order." The Haitian armed forces, which hold the monopoly in law enforcement and security of the country, have become a dangerous force since the departure of Baby Doc. Once he returns from exile after a military coup in February 1991, Jean-Bertrand Aristide wanted to end once and for all the almighty military institution. First, in December 1994, he was trying to weaken it by cutting 1,500 soldiers from its workforce while, on the other hand, he was putting together a police force. We have to underline that the demobilization of more than 75 percent members of the armed forces has enabled the reintegration of less than its half in the interim police force. Second, after publishing the April 1995 decree on the demobilization of the armed forces, he ordered those few soldiers who are still mobilized to integrate the interim police force. Third, in February 1996, the interim police—with its members who are mostly ex-soldiers—was completely dissolved. However, a few hundreds of them, especially former military officers, have become commissioners in the National Police of Haiti (NPH), while the rest—a total of 90 percent of the original force—are not integrated but are still armed.[383]

The DDR program in 1995 is a failure right from the start for the five following reasons. First, the armed forces are destabilized

---

[383] *Supra*, note 289.

because of a spirit of revenge and for personal ambitions; they are not demobilized either with the consent of parliament or with a constitutional amendment. Second, the Armed Forces of Haiti (FAD'H) are public security forces that are legally recognized by the Haitian Constitution of 1987, and they cannot be dismantled by a simple decree and to be replaced later by other forces that are not constitutionally recognized.[384] Third, the ex-military personnel know very well they cannot be discharged without being disarmed, forced to retirement (paid or well remunerated according to the law), or reintegrated into a new public security force. Fourth, by replacing the armed forces by other armed groups and paramilitary forces without following the path of the constitution, the president has declared war or appealed to a civil war between different factions or political spectrum in the country. Finally, popular discontents, armed insurgencies, and a general uprising against a populist dictatorship have now become a point of no return.

6.4.4   The first period of occupation by multinational forces

The fourth period in the Disarmament, Demobilization, and Reintegration (DDR) program is not promising either. In February 2004, after the departure of President Aristide into exile, the Haitian people faced a protectorate of the international community, which was cleared through the Security Council for the deployment of the Interim Multinational Force in Haiti (MIF). The main mission of this security force is to "disarm the 25,000 Haitians in possession of weapons."[385] Unfortunately, it failed for these four following reasons. First, six months is too short for the DDR program. Second, the program allows the purchase of old guns that do not work, while those that can fire bullets are not returned and continue to be used in acts

---

[384] *Supra*, note 332.

[385] *Supra*, note 309.

of banditry. Third, the mission is unable to guarantee public safety. Finally, members of the mission seem to have other motivations to be in Haiti, and they are not willing to risk their lives to solve problems that can be solved by Haitians themselves.

6.4.5   The second period of occupation by multinational forces

Faced with this failure, the Security Council has no choice but to send another multinational force, which—according to its mandate— must provide this time a form of sustainable "security and stability" by giving its full support to the process of reforming the national police. But, caught between the pro-Lavalas armed groups, called Chimères, and paramilitary Duvalierist and neo-Duvalierist forces, the United Nations Mission for Stabilization in Haiti (MINUSTAH)[386] remains in the eyes of most Haitians as the *touristas* mission.[387]

Meanwhile, the Chimères dig their hatchet to organize Operation Baghdad,[388] which forced many sectors of the civilian population to militarize themselves. The multinational force and the Haitian government, faced with this before this fait accompli, enter talks with the young warlords to reduce the chaotic and unsafe risks in

---

[386] New armed forces for the month of January 2008: 7,510 soldiers and 1,750 police officers. *Supra*, note 309.

[387] At the beginning, some members of MINUSTAH preferred to spend a whole day on the beautiful beaches of Haiti, just like the former members of MICIVIH, to have romantic and intimate relationships or to live in cohabitation with Haitians of both sexes. In fact, on November 3, 2007, more than a hundred members of this mission were repatriated to their country of origin after they were accused of sexual abuse of minors and prostitutes.

[388] The National Network for the Defense of Human Rights (RNDDH), in a press release dated September 19, 2006, gives a heavy assessment of this operation: 1,939 people murdered including 108 Haitian police officers, 10 peacekeepers, and 4 journalists; 287 girls and women raped; 500 people kidnapped; 1,241 vehicles stolen.

this country.[389] However, following its renewal,[390] the mission believes now that they are committed to double the pace by moving more in crime prevention. This new orientation reflects not only the Disarmament, Demobilization, and Reintegration (DDR) program but also a comprehensive and adapted program to combat violence based on local conditions; helps initiatives to improve local governance and strengthen the rule of law; provides employment opportunities to former gang members and youth who are at risk; and, finally, collaborates with the Haitian government and the sociopolitical sectors of the country to curb cross-border drugs and weapons trafficking.[391]

Indeed, on this last point, the Inter-American Commission on Human Rights (CHR) suggests that the problem of armed conflict and banditry, which are characterized by systematic violence, is closely related to the proliferation of weapons. According to international authorities, the absence of measures for disarmament or an effective control of the flow of arms to Haiti has perpetuated and exacerbated the violence in the country; the weaknesses of the police presence in Haiti and the serious deficiencies of resources have encouraged illegal armed groups to take control of security in many areas.[392]

This is not surprising, because the commander of the Brazilian troops from the United Nations Mission for Stabilization in Haiti (MINUSTAH), Col. Paolo Umberto, declares the Brazilian peacekeepers were able to check in Cite Soleil and in Cite Militaire the use of large caliber weapons, such as Uzi, Fal Gallil, 12-gauge

---

[389] These young Chimères chiefs are Billy, 2Pac, Evans Ti-Kouto, Amaral Duclonas, Bélony, Dread Wilmer, Ti Bazil, Labanyè, Ti-Blan, Yoyo Piman, and several others.

[390] CS Res. 1702, 15 February 2006.

[391] *Id.*, articles 10, 11 and 13.

[392] Santo Domingo Conference, June 6, 2006. *See* appendix (figure 5).

shotgun, M-15, M-16, and AK-47 by members of armed groups. With this dangerous arsenal, in addition to the amount of ammunition that is available to them, the Disarmament, Demobilization, and Reintegration (DDR) program is and remains inefficient despite its budget.[393]

There is evidence that armed groups involved in violence want to surrender their weapons to be in the DDR program, but they suddenly change their minds, requiring the government to "withdraw the complaints, the cancellation of lawsuits launched against them, the return from exile of President Jean-Bertrand Aristide, the disarmament in the rich neighborhoods, and the cessation of stalking by MINUSTAH of those inhabitants who live in slum cities."[394] It is important to underline that, in 2004, throughout the DDR program by the Interim Multinational Force in Haiti (MIF), these same groups had undertaken several similar tactics not to participate in the program.[395] In fact, they had agreed to surrender their weapons, but they were old guns—called Zam Kreyòl, which are manufactured by their own members—that can no longer function. Later, before and after the elections of February 2006, they decided to lay down their arms but refused to hand them over to authorities. Some leaders, like William Baptiste (a.k.a. Ti-Blanc), declared that those who struggle and participate in this armed movement are not criminals and that, as political combatants, they are entitled to be part of political negotiations.

[393] The mission's annual budget is over $500 million of which $40 million was spent between 2006 and 2007 in the DDR program.

[394] "Haiti-violence: Postponement of handing back the weapons by Cité Soleil gangs," Haitian Press Network, August 21, 2006.

[395] According to the United Nations (UN), these illegal armed groups hold more than twenty thousand firearms. However, ex-soldiers, members of private security companies, and those homes with their own means of defense are not included in this statistic and are said to be in possession of tens of thousands of firearms. See MINUSTAH press briefing notes, August 4, 2005.

This challenging declaration prompted government authorities to change their tone and to issue a clear ultimatum: "Hand over your weapons or die!"[396] Although this ultimatum has some success following the sometimes arbitrary arrests and summary executions,[397] the DDR program is considered a real failure for these five following reasons.[398] First, the National Commission for Disarmament, Demobilization, and Reintegration (NCDDR),[399] whose main purpose is to undertake a general disarmament of all armed groups, has been since its inception able to get back only four hundred large-caliber weapons, while more than two hundred thousand weapons are in circulation.[400] Second, the National Police launches daily wanted notices against some very dangerous people, while the same dangerous people are part of the DDR program and freely go about their daily business without any fear of getting arrested. Third, those individuals who are integrated into the DDR program still have their big guns in their hands and

---

[396] *Statement by President René Préval to armed groups*, August 9, 2006.

[397] Emmanuel "Dread" Wilmer, Charles Junior Acdélhy (alias Yoyo Piman), Thomas Robenson (alias Labanyè), and several others are killed by the national police and the peacekeepers, while others are behind bars: Pierre Belony, Evens Jeune (alias Evens Ti-Kouto), Alain Cadet (alias Pinochè), William Baptiste (alias Ti-blan), Jean Oldy Torchon (alias Blade Nasson), Bazile Soijette (alias Ti-bazile), and some of their lieutenants. Amaral Duclonas, meanwhile, is still on the run.

[398] We must note, according to the United Nations (UN), the confusion around the concept of DDR in Haiti: the conditions for the execution of a credible DDR program are not met, and the political framework necessary for the development of this type of program is also nonexistent for now. See MINUSTAH press briefing notes, August 4, 2005.

[399] Created by the Presidential Decree of August 29, 2006. According to Alix Fils-Aimé, president of the commission, a total of five hundred individuals, between seventeen and twenty-four years old, are currently attending vocational courses as part of the DDR program and are on the verge to be reintegrated into society.

[400] Robert MUGGAH, *Securing Haiti's Transition: Reviewing Human Insecurity and the Prospects for Disarmament, Demobilization, and Reintegration*, Small Arms Survey, October 2005.

continue to commit horrendous crimes (kidnappings, murders, armed robberies, and rapes).[401] Fourth, a representative of the commission is well known as Jean-Baptiste Jean Philippe (a.k.a. Samba Boukman), an individual who threatened the population of the metropolitan area as well as the authorities themselves, and he was the main spokesperson of the Chimères during Operation Baghdad.[402] And, finally, although the commission states that it attaches particular importance to children who are the main victims of armed groups, the DDR program contains no reliable system to truly rehabilitate these children.

Indeed, these children—who are associated with armed groups, who have witnessed atrocities, or who have seen their parents killed, injured, or raped—are much in need of psychosocial support to overcome their problems. The multiple interventions of the United Nations Children's Fund (UNICEF), despite having maintained learning programs, sensitization workshops on child rights, and training sessions,[403] are not sufficient for these children to turn their back permanently to crime to become good citizens of the society so they could take control of their lives. In fact, what can these interventions do when these poor children are able to wield Kalashnikovs and T-65 with equal dexterity that can easily and

---

[401] According to the president of the DDR Commission, 10 percent of the individuals who are integrated into the program are repeat offenders. For example, Patrick Jean François—a former beneficiary of the program—has been actively wanted by the police since January 26, 2008, for kidnapping and attempted murder against the person of Claude Marcelin, a well-known guitarist of the musical group Zèklè.

[402] *Supra*, note 388.

[403] The United Nations Children's Fund (UNICEF) also provides assistance to government institutions for the protection of children, including the Institute for Social Welfare and Research (IBESR), the Brigade for the Protection of Minors of the Haitian National Police (PNH), the Office for Citizen Protection (OPC), and the Children's Courts.

quickly earn them a living?[404] What can those interventions do when the leaders of armed gangs, who are now reformed into a new group known as the Argentins, give automatic weapons to children of ten, twelve, and thirteen years old and who still share their environment and live in the same slum?[405]

By contrast, if these interventions provide economic relief to these children, they are only temporary. For many reasons, the physical and sexual abuse those children experienced left emotional scars that, if they are not supported,[406] will perpetuate and transform later into other acts of violence.[407] Moreover, within the legal framework of children in conflict with the law,[408] the Haitian government is unable by itself to fix this problem. The lack of expertise in the field of Haitian juvenile delinquency and the administration of juvenile justice is a handicap.

---

[404] These are the words of the president of the National DDR Commission.

[405] Edmond Mulet, civilian head of MINUSTAH and special representative of Kofi Annan (secretary general of the United Nations), says he has seen leaders of armed gangs give weapons to children.

[406] According to the branch of UNICEF in Haiti, the issue of children involved in armed violence is a very important issue regarding the care and possibly the social and family reintegration of these children who are seriously affected by the conflict. However, UNICEF has not given any explanation or exact description of the term "care." *Cf.* Interview with Njanja FASSU, official representative of UNICEF, in "Discussion workshop as a prelude to the National Day of Children involved in Violence: Education and Social Reintegration of Children involved in Violence in Haiti," National Television of Haiti, June 8, 2006.

[407] Diego Lambert (alias Ti-Diégo), a fifteen-year-old teenager (thirteen years old at the time of the crime), was arrested by the police for having been involved in the kidnapping of Farah Natacha Kerby Dessources in November 2006. According to the police, the alleged kidnapper would have confessed to having put out both eyes of the young woman (aged twenty) before his gang killed her. *See* Haiti-Banditisme, RadioKiskeya.com, January 11, 2008.

[408] The law of September 7, 1961, and the decree of November 20, 1961, provide specific measures and procedures applicable to minors under sixteen regarding criminal matters.

In fact, in Haiti, the minimum age of criminal responsibility of a child is thirteen years old, while the age of criminal majority is sixteen.[409] However, the Haitian judicial system contains no real mechanism—although laws are written—that could positively affect the lives of these children and could enable them one day to enjoy fully their fundamental rights in relation to health care, education and legal services, and civil and social rights. We know that the international community has pledged to adopt "feasible measures"[410] to prevent armed groups from recruiting or not using children under eighteen years of age in armed conflicts.[411] We also know that the international community wants to "fight against impunity, investigate and effectively prosecute anyone who have unlawfully recruited children under the age of 18 in armed forces or groups."[412]

Finally, we know that the same international community wants to "discuss, reflect and support the government [of Haiti] in finding solutions to the involvement of children in armed violence."[413] However, can we say—as many believe—that their position would almost be to leave for tomorrow today's problems like a futile exercise that is embedded in a social humanitarian posture?[414]

---

[409] Articles 50 to 52 of the Penal Code establish a specific penal statute for children aged thirteen to sixteen, and this will depend on cases of less seriousness and under certain circumstances. If the children are under twelve and are guilty of a crime, the juvenile judge may resort to measures of protection, supervision, assistance, or education.

[410] Legal and administrative measures.

[411] *Paris Commitments*, 6 February 2007.

[412] *Id.*, article 6.

[413] *Supra*, note 406. See Njanja FASSU's interview.

[414] Jean-Claude BAJEUX, "The Crossroads of Transcendence," Port-au-Prince, Ecumenical Center for Human Rights, 24 May 2006.

CONCLUSION

Treating the problem of child soldiers is particularly important when this approach aims to ensure that international law focuses on the criminal responsibility of the child soldier. The goal is not to criminalize the child [aggressor] but to stop the systemic recruitment of children and prevent the systematic delinquency of ex-child combatants. As the Swiss MP Jean-Paul Glasson stated so well, "Childhood is the period during which human being sets his bearings, learn about life and its values."[415] Clearly, we have no doubt about this. However, international law seems to give a "special protection" for child soldiers who were involved in crimes against humanity and genocide, so those "benchmarks" are not clear.

The history of the Spartan children, the Mamluks of Egypt, the La Flèche Cadets, or the Lebensborn of Hitler is not so different from the history of the Iranian Bassidji, the African Kadogos, the Mara Salvatrucha from El Salvador, and the children of the Haitian Chimères. These stories show that children are often used for personal purposes, but they can also decide on their own volition and become conscripts to satisfy their personal interests. In fact, the problem of children recruited into armed forces and paramilitary groups is a global scourge that the international humanitarian law and international law of human rights are unable to resolve, especially when there is ambiguity over the dual legal status of child soldiers who are seen as victims rather than aggressors. Despite that there is no confusion in the definition of these terms,[416] we see a paradox when a

---

[415] *Parliamentary initiative: Organized crime against children is a crime against humanity*, National Council of the Swiss Parliament, 19 June 2003.

[416] A victim is any person who has suffered harm that violates the laws, while an aggressor is any individual who, as a leader or organizer (may be in the

child is both a victim and an aggressor. In this sense, international law wants to ignore this paradox to let us believe that a child cannot be an aggressor when he is a victim. Thus, if we must consider the child as a victim, what happened to his victims, and where do they go? Do we have to ignore the thousands of people who are killed, maimed, raped, and tortured?

Indeed, the incoherence of international law to rule on the legal aspect of the child soldier who is a victim and a perpetrator is closely linked to a malaise that is based on a calculated and deliberate conventional decision regarding the legal concept that the child who is under eighteen years is a minor, he cannot be held accountable for his actions, and that, if there is any, he must have a special treatment or protection. It is a perfect contradiction when a child can "voluntarily" enlist in the armed forces and "indirectly" participate in hostilities, while that same child can rape, torture, and kill at will and still be accepted as a victim of war as a result of armed conflict. It is also a contradiction when a child, who is a "commander," leads an armed group, among which there are adults who are under his command and were ordered to torture and execute people, when that same "commander" cannot be tried for crimes against humanity because of his legal status as a child soldier, a casualty of war. It was believed that the Principles of the Rome Statute, the 1674 Resolution of the Security Council of the United Nations, and the Rules and Procedures of the International Criminal Court prohibit any amnesty and would require every government to prosecute all perpetrators of crimes against humanity, crimes of genocide, and massive violations of international human rights. Is it not that the Protocol I to the Geneva Convention protects children against their recruitment and their involvement in armed conflict, and the Optional Protocol to

---

service of a group or an agent of a government), takes an active part in—or directs—the planning, preparation, initiation, or conduct of an aggression.

the Convention on the Rights of the child accepts that children who are fifteen years old can be recruited voluntarily into armed forces or armed groups, of course with the consent of their parents, as well as not indirectly participate in hostilities?

Thus, if the child can be enrolled voluntarily in the military, participate indirectly in hostilities, and commit war crimes and crimes against humanity, why is he not brought before the International Criminal Court? This inconsistency on the dual legal status of the child soldier also arises in article 38 of the Convention on the Rights of the Child, which allows the recruitment of children under eighteen. There would not be any problem in placing a child aggressor before a special court. This is not to punish the child again but to ensure that the administration of juvenile justice is effective when the law of a country has no reliable system of justice. What is disturbing is when the international community recognizes that the domestic law of some countries is outmoded and that it refuses to take charge of a case while knowing that the management of this case by the domestic authorities shall do prejudice to the fundamental rights of the accused.[417] Another problem arises when we do not accept that the child soldier is an aggressor; it is becoming a systematic delinquency of children by their simple involvement in crimes, and it is also the best opportunity for recruiters to automatically recruit more children, while both recruiters and aggressors are enjoying impunity freely without having fear of being held accountable.

Impunity, particularly fatal to the victims of atrocities, stems from our inability to punish the perpetrators, especially in a country like Haiti, "the only country in the world where we judge no one,

---

[417] This is the case of Babuya Oleko, a child soldier who was arrested on November 15, 2000, and sentenced to death on January 10, 2001, for murder. Babuya Oleko arrived on July 20, 2001, at Kinshasa central prison, where he is imprisoned with adult death row inmates.

a country that is in a weakened state to try, to condemn violence, murder, drug trafficking[418] and corruption."[419] In a nonindustrialized country where there never was a social transformation, because this transformation is prevented by social problems and politico-economic conflicts that often lead to armed conflicts, the concept of legal protection of children is purely philosophical, especially with problems in accepting the conventions of international humanitarian law and international law of human rights. Furthermore, if these countries do not adhere to a convention, it will be impossible to hold them accountable for the violations of human rights and humanitarian law.[420]

This inconsistent attitude of the international community about the dual legal status of child soldiers gave the impression that the child will always be considered a victim. But, according to many, "what are the peacekeepers doing, deprived of offensive weapons, sent here and there without any real written rules and agree to be bombed? The charade of international order is not fooling anyone. Quite the contrary, it frustrates the masses by making them hope for a form of worldwide justice [and democracy]."[421] In fact, for others, "to address

---

[418] Selon la Télévision Nationale d'Haïti (TNH), la police a saisit le 23 août 2006 près de 372 kilos de According to the National Television of Haiti (TNH), the police seized on August 23, 2006, nearly 372 kilos of cocaine, which is valued on the mastiff market at $8,184,000, including $22,000 per kilo. The authorities of the National Police of Haiti (PNH), particularly the police chief Mario Andrésol, believe that the armed conflict and violence in general are linked to drugs and the proliferation of weapons.

[419] *Supra*, note 414.

[420] We must admit that apart from any international convention, especially when it comes to internal or noninternational armed conflicts, states must comply with certain customary rules. See: Jean-Marie HENCKAERTS and Louise DOSWALD-BECK, "Customary International Humanitarian Law," Cambridge, Cambridge University Press, vol. 3, 2005.

[421] WAKI, "International Law: A Beautiful Chimera," Agora Vox, 14 August 2006.

the senseless violence and destruction syndrome, we must begin by opposing [child soldiers], without any hesitation, the force of law, the transcendence of Justice,"[422] especially with the new 1674 Resolution; hopefully, it will bind the Security Council in a more systematic way, such as in situations of crisis, in foreign peacekeeping missions that are more integrated, a strengthened humanitarian response, and the establishment of more effective legal recourse in many places to end suffering and impunity.

---

[422] *Supra*, note 414.

APPENDIX

Figure 1 – The child and the age of reason

Percentage of correct answers in three of the relevant conditions on the quantifiers (taken from Noveck, 2001, Experiment 3)			
	8 years	10 years	Adults
True existential affirmations Ex. *Some birds live in cages.*	84%	90%	99%
Universal false statements Ex. *All the children are blond.*	86%	99%	96%
True but inappropriate existential claims Ex. *Some elephants have trunks.*	89%	85%	41%

Figure 2 – Table of international and transnational legislation

International Organizations	International Instruments (Conventions, Declarations and Treaties)	Date of Adoption	Date of Entry into force
United Nations	Universal Declaration of Human Rights	10/12/1948	S/O
	Convention relating to the Status of Refugees	28/07/1951	22/04/1954
	Declaration of the Rights of the Child	20/11/1959	S/O
	International Covenant on Civil and Political Rights	16/12/1966	23/03/1976
	Convention against Torture and Other Cruel, Inhuman, or Degrading Treatment or Punishment	10/12/1984	26/06/1987
	Minimum Rules for the Administration of Juvenile Justice (Beijing Rules)	29/11/1985	S/O
	Convention on the Rights of the Child	20/11/1989	2/09/1990
	Minimum rules for the development of nonpreventive liberty measures (Tokyo rules)	14/12/1990	S/O
	Rules for the protection of minors deprived of their liberty	14/12/1990	S/O
	Guiding Principles for the Prevention of Juvenile Delinquency (Riyadh Guiding Principles)	14/12/1990	S/O
	Principles concerning the status and functioning of national institutions for the protection and promotion of human rights (Paris principles)	3/03/1992	20/12/1993
	Vienna Guidelines on Children in the Criminal Justice System	21/07/1997	S/O

International Organizations	International Instruments (Conventions, Declarations and Treaties)	Date of Adoption	Date of Entry into force
United Nations	Declaration of Basic Principles of Justice for Victims of Crime and Abuse of Power	29/11/1985	S/O
	Guidelines on Justice for Child Victims and Witnesses of Crime	21/07/2004	S/O
	Statute (of Rome) of the International Criminal Court	17/07/1998	11/04/2002
	Statute of the Special Court for Sierra Leone	14/08/2000	16/01/2002
	Optional Protocol to the Convention on the Rights of the Child on the Involvement of Children in Armed Conflict	25/05/2000	22/02/2002
	Basic and Guiding Principles Concerning the Right to a Remedy and Reparation for Victims of Gross Violations of International Human Rights Law and Serious Violations of International Humanitarian Law	21/03/2006	S/O
Organization of American States	American Declaration of the Rights and Duties of Man	2/05/1948	S/O
	American Convention on Human Rights	22/11/1969	18/07/1978
European Union	European Convention of Human Rights	4/11/1950	3/09/1953
Council of Europe[423]	European social charter	18/10/1961	1/07/1999

---

[423] The charter was revised on May 3, 1996.

International Organizations	International Instruments (Conventions, Declarations and Treaties)	Date of Adoption	Date of Entry into force
International Committee of the Red Cross	Geneva Conventions (I, II, III and IV)	12/08/1949	21/10/1950
	Additional Protocol I relating to the protection of victims of international armed conflicts	8/06/1977	7/12/1978
	Additional Protocol II relating to the protection of victims of international armed conflicts	8/06/1977	7/12/1978
African Union	African Charter on the Rights and Welfare of the Child	11/07/1990	29/11/1999
International Labor Organization	Convention on the Abolition of Forced Labor	25/06/1957	17/01/1959
	Worst Forms of Child Labor Convention	1/06/1999	19/11/2000
	Minimum age convention	26/06/1973	19/06/1976

Figure 3 – Table of national legislation

Member States	National Instruments	Date of Adoption/ Entry in force
United States of America[424]	Fair Labor Standards Act, 29 USC § 212	1938
	Criminal Procedure Act, 18 USC § 1401	1964
	Racketeer Influenced and Corrupt Organization Act (RICO), 18 USC § 96	1968
	Violent Crime Control and Law Enforcement Act, 18 USC §§ 113 (a), (b) and (c), 1111, 1113, §§ 2111, 2113 and 2241	1994
Republic of Benin	Juvenile Justice and Delinquency Act, 42 USC § 5601	2002
	Ordinance relating to the judgment of offenses committed by minors under 18, N°69-23/PR/MJL	10/07/1969
Colombia	Code for Youth	1989
	Law 49-99 on military service	1999
Democratic Republic of Congo	Decree on delinquency	6/12/1950
	Decree No. 066 on the demobilization of children enlisted in the armed forces	9/06/2000
Republic of Haiti	Juvenile Justice Administration Act	7/09/1961
	Labor Code	12/09/1961
	Decree on the administration of juvenile justice	20/11/1961
	Decree amending the Penal Code of 1836	23/05/1985
	Decree updating the Labor Code of 1961	24/02/1994
	National Police Law	29/11/1994
	Decree amending the 1995 electoral law	23/03/1999
Nicaragua	Labor Code (reform)	1997
	Childhood and Adolescence Code	1998

---

[424] The United States of America is a member of the UN but has not ratified (as has Somalia) the Convention on the Rights of the Child. However, these two countries signed this convention on February 16, 1995, and May 9, 2002, respectively.

Member States	National Instruments	Date of Adoption/ Entry in force
Islamic Republic of Pakistan	Penal Code	1960
	Juvenile Justice System Ordinance	2000
	Ordinances relating to Zina and Hadood	1979
Republic of Sierra Leone	Rules of customary law or traditional practices	S/O
	Sierra Leonean Citizenship Law	1973
Republic of Uganda	Status of Children Act	1996
Canada (Province of Quebec)	Act to amend the Youth Protection Act	2001

Figure 4 – Case law table

Member states	Description	N° du dossier	Date
Angola	Child soldier: executions of young people	452653 (UNHCR)	28/05/2004
Colombia	Committee Concluding Observations	CRC/C/15/Add.137	16/10/2000
Congo (DRC)	*Babuyu Oleko v. the DRC Military Order Court*	E/CN.4/2002/74/Add.2	8/05/2002
El Salvador	Committee Concluding Observations	CRC/C/15/Add.9	18/10/1993
Haiti	Committee Concluding Observations	CRC/C/15/Add.202	18/03/2003
Liberia	Committee Concluding Observations	CRC/C/15/Add.236	1/07/2004
Nicaragua	Committee Concluding Observations	CRC/C/15/Add.108	24/08/1999
Ouganda	Committee Concluding Observations	CRC/C/15/Add.80	21/10/1997
Pakistan	Committee Concluding Observations	CRC/C/15/Add.217	27/10/2003
Sierra Leone	Committee Concluding Observations	CRC/C/15/Add.116	24/02/2000
Soudan	Committee Concluding Observations	CRC/C/15/Add.190	9/10/2002

Figure 5 – Haiti: international and transnational conventions and treaties

Date of Admission to UN: 24 October 1945; to **OAS**: 30 April 1948; to **CARICOM**: 3 July 2002

Treaty	Status	Signature Date	Ratification or Accession Date	Reporting Record
Convention on the Rights of the Child (UN)	Ratification	26.01.1990	08.06.1995	Initial report 03.04.2001
Optional Protocol to the Convention on the Rights of the Child on the Involvement of Children in Armed Conflict (UN)		15.08.2002		
Optional to the Convention on the Rights of the Child on the Sale of Children, Child Protection and Child Pornography (UN)		15.08.2002		
Convention on the Elimination of all Forms of Racial Discrimination (UN)	Ratification	30.10.1972	19.12.1972	Initial report 20.05.1974
International Covenant on Civil and Political Rights (UN)	Accession		06.02.1991	Special report 27.02.1995
Convention on the Elimination of all Forms of Discrimination against Women (UN)	Ratification	17.07.1980	20.07.1981	
Covenant on the Political Rights of Women (UN)	Ratification	23.07.1957	12.02.1958	
Convention related to the Status of Refugees (UN)	Accession		25.09.1984	
Protocol relating to the Status of Refugees (UN)	Accession		25.09.1984	

Treaty	Status	Signature Date	Ratification or Accession Date	Reporting Record
Convention against Illicit Traffic in Narcotics, Drugs and Psychotropic Substances (UN)	Accession		18.09.1995	
Protocol related to the Convention against Illicit Traffic in Narcotics, Drugs and Psychotropic Substances (UN)	Accession		18.09.1995	
Convention for Limiting the Manufacture and Regulating the Distribution of Narcotic Drugs (UN)		31.05.1951		
Protocol to Prevent, Suppress and Punish Trafficking in Persons, Especially Women and Children (UN)		13.12.2000		
Convention on the Prevention and Punishment of the Crime of Genocide (UN)	Ratification	11.12.1948	14.10.1950	
Rome Statute of the International Criminal Court (UN/ICRC)		26.02.1999		
Charter of the Organization of American States (OAS)	Ratification	30.04.1948	21.08.1950	
American Convention on Human Rights (OAS)	Accession		14.09.1977	
Additional Protocol to the American Convention on Human Rights in the area of Economic, Social and Cultural Rights (OAS)		17.11.1988		
Inter-American Convention to Prevent and Punish Torture (OAS)		13.06.1986		

Treaty	Status	Signature Date	Ratification or Accession Date	Reporting Record
Inter-American Convention on the Return of Minors (OAS)		15.07.1989		
Inter-American Convention on the Conflict of Laws concerning the Adoption of Minors (OAS)		24.05.1984		
Inter-American Convention on the Granting of Civil Rights to Women (OAS)		02.05.1948		
Inter-American Convention on the Granting of Political Rights to Women (OAS)	Ratification	01.98.1957	21.10.1957	
Inter-American Convention on the Prevention, Punishment and Eradication of Violence Against Women (OAS)	Accession		07.04.1997	
Inter-American Convention Against Terrorism (OAS)		03.06.2002		
Inter-American Treaty of Reciprocal Assistance (OAS)	Ratification	02.09.1947	30.10.1947	
Inter-American Convention on Extradition (OAS)		25.02.1981		
Inter-American Convention Against Corruption (OAS)	Ratification	29.03.1996	14.04.2004	
Convention concerning the Hours of Work (ILO/C-1)	Ratification		31.03.1952	
Convention on the Minimum Age (Industry) (ILO/C-5)	Ratification		12.04.1957	
Convention on Workmen's Compensation concerning Accidents (ILO/C-17)	Ratification		19.04.1955	
Convention on Forced Labour (Agriculture) (ILO/C-25)	Ratification		04.03.1958	

Treaty	Status	Signature Date	Ratification or Accession Date	Reporting Record
Convention concerning the Freedom of Association and Protection of the Right to Organize (ILO/C-87)	Ratification		05.06.1979	
Convention concerning the Night Work of Young Persons (ILO/C-90)	Ratification		12.04.1957	
Convention concerning the Right to Organize and Collective Bargaining (ILO/C-98)	Ratification		12.04.1957	
Convention on Equal Remuneration (ILO/C-100)	Ratification		04.03.1958	
Convention concerning the Abolition of Forced Labour (ILO/C-105)	Ratification		04.03.1958	
Convention on Discrimination (Employment and Occupation) (ILO/C-111)	Ratification		09.11.1976	

Figure 6 – Haiti and armed groups

Armed Groups	Description	Movements	Date in Function
Caciquats	Anti-colonial (Kingdom of Spain)	Antislavery and revolutionary	1492–1560
Marrons	Anti-colonial (Spain and France)	Antislavery and revolutionary	1560–1802
Bossales	Anti-colonial (Spain and France)	Antislavery and revolutionary	1698–1802
Congos	Anti-colonial (Spain and France)	Antislavery and revolutionary	1692–1802
Armée Révolutionnaire	Anti-colonial (Kingdom of France)	Antislavery and revolutionary	1802–1806
Armée de l'Ouest	Pro-governmental (Alexandre Pétion)	Anti-northerner and anti-insurgency	1807–1818
Armée du Nord	Pro-governmental (Henri Christophe)	Anti-southerner and anti-insurgency	1807–1820
Armée Souffrante	Anti-governmental (Rivière Hérard)	Revolutionary	1844
Piquets	Anti-governmental (Rivière Hérard and his successors)	Revolutionary, anti-insurgency, and criminal	1844–1870
Zinglins	Pro-governmental (Rivière Hérard and his successors)	Anti-insurgency and criminal	1844–1867
Cacos	Anti-governmental (Rivière Hérard and his successors) and anti-imperialist (USA)	Revolutionary, anti-insurgency, and criminal	1844–1920
Young people from La Saline and Bel-Air	Pro-governmental (Daniel Fignolé)	Insurgency: Compressor Roller	1954–1957
Cagoulards	Pro-governmental (François Duvalier)	Anti-insurgency and criminal	1957–1959
Civilian Militia "Tonton Macoutes"	Pro-governmental (François Duvalier)	Revolutionary, anti-insurgency, and criminal	1959–1964
Volontaires de la Sécurité Nationale (VSN)	Pro-governmental (François Duvalier and Jean Claude Duvalier)	Anti-insurgency and criminal	1964–1986

Armed Groups	Description	Movements	Date in Function
Fillettes Laleau	Pro-governmental (François Duvalier and Jean Claude Duvalier)	Anti-insurgency and criminal	1965–1986
Communistes	Anti-governmental (The Opposition)	Revolutionary	1960–1986
Kamoken	Anti-governmental (The Opposition)	Revolutionary	1962–1984
Unknown (many political parties)	Anti-governmental (Jean-Claude Duvalier)	Revolutionary and criminal: Cesarean and decoukage operations	1980–1986
Brigades de Vigilance	Anti-governmental (Military Juntas)	Insurgency and criminal: Decoukage Operations	1986–1994
Brassards Rouges	Pro-governmental (Military Juntas)	Anti-insurgency and criminal	1988
Zenglendos	Pro-governmental (Military Juntas)	Anti-insurgency and criminal	1988–1991
Attachés	Pro-governmental (Military Juntas)	Anti-insurgency and criminal	1991–1994
Organisations Populaires (OP)	Pro-governmental (J.-B. Aristide and Rene Preval)	Revolutionary and criminal: Decoukage Operations and Rache Manyòk	1991–2006
Escadrons de la Mort	Pro-governmental (Military Juntas)	Anti-insurgency and criminal	1992–1994
FRAPH	Pro-governmental (Military Juntas)	Anti-insurgency and criminal	1993–1995
5ᵉ Colonne	Pro-governmental (J.-B. Aristide)	Anti-insurgency and criminal	2001–2006
Armée Sans Manman	Anti-governmental (J.-B. Aristide)	Insurrectional and criminal	2002–2004
Armée Rat	Pro-governmental (J.-B. Aristide)	Anti-insurgency and criminal	2003–2006
Armée Cannibale	Pro-governmental and anti-governmental (J.-B. Aristide)	Anti-insurrectional and criminal: Punch Operation	2001–2004
Armée Rouge	Pro-governmental (J.-B. Aristide)	Revolutionary and criminal	1994–2006

Armée Saddam Hussein	Pro-governmental (J.-B. Aristide)	Anti-insurgency and criminal	2001–2006
Dòmi Nan Bwa	Pro-governmental (J.-B. Aristide)	Anti-insurgency and criminal	2001–2005
Bale Wouze	Pro-governmental (J.-B. Aristide)	Anti-insurgency and criminal	2001–2005
Base Pilate	Pro-governmental (J.-B. Aristide)	Anti-insurgency and criminal	2003–2008
Base Grand Ravine	Pro-governmental (J.-B. Aristide)	Anti-insurgency and criminal	2003–2008
Soré - Martissant	Pro-governmental (J.-B. Aristide)	Anti-insurgency and criminal	2003–2008
Ti Bois	Pro-governmental (J.-B. Aristide)	Anti-insurgency and criminal	2003–2008
Armée Ti-Manchèt	Pro-governmental (Gérard Latortue)	Anti-insurgency and criminal	2004–2008
FRN	Anti-governmental (J.-B. Aristide)	Revolutionary	2004–2006
Cercueil	Pro-governmental (J.-B. Aristide)	Anti-insurgency and criminal	2001–2004
Kokorat	Pro-governmental (J.-B. Aristide)	Anti-insurgency and criminal	2002–2006
Ratpakaka	Pro-governmental (J.-B. Aristide)	Anti-insurgency and criminal	2002–2006
RAMICOS	Anti-governmental (J.-B. Aristide)	Insurgency	2001–2007
Chimères	Pro-governmental (J.-B. Aristide)	Revolutionary, anti-insurgency, and criminal: Baghdad Operations I and II	2001–2008

BIBLIOGRAPHY

1.0 Ouvrages juridiques:

- ACHOUR, R. B., S. LAGHMANI (dir.), *Harmonie et Contradictions en droit international*, Paris, Éditions A. Pedone, 1996, 346 p.

- ARZOUMANIAN, N. et F. PIZZUTELLI, « Victimes et bourreaux: questions de responsabilité liées à la problématique des enfants–soldats en Afrique », (2003) 85 R.I.C.R. 827

- BAZELAIRE, J.-P. et T. CRETIN, *La justice pénale internationale: son évolution, son avenir: de Nuremberg à la Haye*, Paris, Presses Universitaires de France, 2000, 261 p.

- BOUCHET-SAULNIER, F., *Dictionnaire pratique du droit humanitaire*, Paris, La Découverte & Syros, 2000, 492 p.

- COALITION TO STOP THE USE OF CHILD SOLDIERS, *Child soldiers: global report 2001*, Londres, Child soldiers, 2001, 452 p.

- *Jurisprudence on the rights of the child*, t. 3, by COHEN, C. P., Ardsley, Transnational Publishers Inc., 2005, 530 p.

- COHN, I. et G. GOODWIN-GILL (dir.), *Enfant-soldat: le rôle des enfants dans les conflits armés*, Montréal, Éditions du Méridien, 1995, 267 p.

- COMITÉ INTERNATIONAL DE LA CROIX-ROUGE, *Les enfants dans la guerre*, Genève, CIRC, 2004, 67 p.

- DAVID, E., *Code de droit international pénal*, Bruxelles, Éditions Bruylant, 2004, 1532 p.

- DAVID, E., F. TULKENS, et D. VANDERMEERSCH, *Code de droit international humanitaire*, Bruxelles, Bruylant, 2004, 860 p.

- De SCHUTTER, O., F. TULKENS et S. V. DROOGHENBROECK, *Code de droit international des droits de l'homme*, Bruxelles, Bruylant, 2000, 526 p.

- FOUSSENI, S., *La responsabilité pénale des enfants soldats*, Paris, Université de Nantes (Paris X), 2004, 67 p.

- GRADITZKY, T., « La responsabilité pénale individuelle pour violation du droit international humanitaire applicable en situation de conflit armé non international », (1998) 21 R.I.C.R. 829

- HARVEY, R., *Children and armed conflict: a guide to international humanitarian and human rights law*, Essex, University of Essex, 2003, 92 p.

- HAUT COMMISSARIAT DES NATIONS UNIES POUR LES RÉFUGIÉS, *La violence sexuelle et sexiste contre les réfugiés, les rapatriés et les personnes déplacées: Principes directeurs pour la prévention et l'intervention*, New York, Nations Unies, 2003, 182 p.

- HUMAN RIGHTS WATCH, *La guerre dans la guerre: Violence sexuelle contre les femmes et les filles dans l'est du Congo*, Brussels, HRW, 2002, 62 p.

- INSTITUT INTERNATIONAL DES DROITS DE L'ENFANT, *L'enfant et la guerre,* Genève, Institut Universitaire Kurt Bosch, 2001, 162 p.

- LLUELLES, D., *Guide des références pour la rédaction juridique*, Montréal, Éditions Thémis, 2000, 202 p.

- RENAUT, C., *L'interdiction de recruter des enfants soldats*, Paris, Centre de recherches et d'études sur les droits de l'Homme et le droit humanitaire, Université Paris Sud (Paris XI), 2000, 60 p.

- RUBELLIN-DEVICHI, J. et R. FRANK (dir.), *L'enfant et les conventions internationales*, Lyon, Presses Universitaires, 1996, 492 p.

- SALMON, J., (dir.), *Dictionnaire de droit international public*, Bruxelles, Éditions Bruylant, 2001, 1198 p.
- UNITED CHILDREN'S FUND, *The state of the world's children in 2005: Childhood under threat*, New York, Unicef House, 2004, 164 p.

1.1 Ouvrages non-juridiques:

- ABBOTT, E., « Haiti: The Duvaliers and Their Legacy », New York, McGraw-Hill Book Company, 1988, 382 p.
- ACHILLE, T., « Aristide: le dire et le faire », Montréal, Les Éditions de la Vérité, 1998, 118 p.
- ARISTIDE, J.-B., « Theology and Politics », Montréal, Les Éditions du CIDIHCA, 1995, 132 p.
- BADJOKO, L. et K. CLARENS, *J'étais Enfant-soldat: le récit poignant d'une enfance africaine*, Paris, Éditions Plon, 2005, 162 p.
- BEA, I., « A Long Way Gone: Memoirs of a Boy Soldier », New York, Farrar, Straus and Giroux, 2007, 240 p.
- BERTRAND, M., (dir.), *Les enfants dans la guerre et les violences civiles: Approches cliniques et théoriques*, Paris, Éditions L'Harmattan, 1997, 159 p.
- BOLYA, *La profanation des vagins: le viol comme arme de guerre et arme de destruction massive*, Paris, Éditions Le Serpent à Plumes, 2002, 201 p.
- BONNARDOT, M.-L. et DANROC, G., « La chute de la maison Duvalier: Textes pour l'histoire », Montréal, Éditions KARTHALA, 1989, 320 p.
- BOYDEN, J. and J. BERRY (dir.), *Children and youth on the front line: ethnography, armed conflict and displacement*, New York, Bergham Books, 2004, 274 p.
- BRETT, R. and I. SPECHT, *Young soldiers: why they choose to fight*, Boulder, Lynne Rienner Publishers Inc., 2004, 192 p.

- CORTEN, A., « Diabolisation et Mal Politique. Haïti: misère, religion et politique », Montréal, Les Éditions du CIDHICA-KARTHALA, 2000, 246 p.

- De LACROIX, P. et PLUCHON, P., *La révolution de Haïti*, t.1 et 2, « Mémoires pour servir à l'histoire de la révolution de Saint-Domingue », 2ᵉ éd. par P. Pluchon, Paris, Éditions KARTHALA, 1995, 528 p.

- DHÔTEL, G., *Les enfants dans la guerre*, coll. « Les Essentiels Milan », Toulouse, Éditions Milan, 1999, 63 p.

- DORSAINVIL, J.-C., « Manuel d'Histoire d'Haïti », Port-au-Prince, Imprimerie Henri Deschamps, 1924, 372 p.

- ENGLISH, A. D., « Understanding Military Culture: A Canadian Perspective », Montreal, McGill-Queen's University Press, 2004, 198 p.

- FERGUSON, J., « Papa Doc, Baby Doc: Haiti and the Duvaliers », New York, Basil Blackwell Ltd, 1987, 172 p.

- HEINL, R. D. and HEINL, N. G., « Written in Blood - The Story of the Haitian People: 1492-1971 », Boston, Houghton Mifflin Company, 1978, 786 p.

- KEITETSI, C., *La petite fille à la kalachnikov: ma vie d'Enfant-soldat*, Bruxelles, Éditions GRIP, 2004, 265 p.

- LANEYRIE-DAGEN, N., *Les grands événements de l'histoire des enfants*, coll. « La Mémoire de l'humanité », Paris, Édition Larousse, 1995, 320 p.

- MOISE, C., *Constitutions et luttes de pouvoir en Haïti*, t. 1, « 1804-1915: La faillite des classes dirigeantes », Montréal, Les Éditions du CIDIHCA, 1988, 340 p.

- MOISE, C., *Constitutions et luttes de pouvoir en Haïti*, t. 2, « 1915-1987: De l'occupation étrangère à la dictature macoute », Montréal, Les Éditions du CIDIHCA, 1990, 570 p.

- OSSEIRAN-HOUBBALLAH, M., *L'Enfant-soldat: victime transformée en bourreau*, Paris, Odile Jacob, 2003, 233 p.
- SANSARICQ, B., « Le pouvoir de la foi », Montréal, Éditions Du Marais, 2006, 394 p.
- SCHMITZ, M. et O. A. OTUNNU (dir.), *La guerre: enfants admis*, Bruxelles, Éditions GRIP, 2001, 184 p.
- SINGER, P. W., *Children at war*, New York, Pantheon Books, 2005, 269 p.

1.2 Sources multimédia (Internet, documentaires et autres documents visuels):

- AMNESTY INTERNATIONAL, «Libéria: Les promesses de la paix pour 21,000 enfants soldats», Londres, mai 2004 http://web.amnesty.org/library/Index/FRAAFR340062004?open&of=FRA-364
- AMNESTY INTERNATIONAL, « République Démocratique du Congo: enfants en guerre », Secrétariat International, 9 septembre 2003 http://web.amnesty.org/report2006/index-fra
- CORNELLIER, R., P. HENRIQUEZ et R. PROVENCHER, « Enfance assassinée », Macumba International (Série Extremis, Télé-Québec), 2001
- «Darfur peace plan signed by one rebel group: Two others refuse; U.N. chief says force may be needed to protect civilians », Associated Press, 5 May 2006 http://www.msnbc.msn.com/id/12627670/
- DARMEL, J., « Justice Haïtienne: affaire Jean Yves Noël », Haitian Promotional Group for Democracy, 24 mai 2006 http://groups.yahoo.com/group/Haitianpolitics/message/41543
- DAVIS, P., « Hearts and Minds », Janus Films, 1974
- DEMME, J., « The Agronomist », New Line Home Video, 2005

- HUMAN RIGHTS WATCH, « Le chef des Janjaweed affirme que le gouvernement soudanais a soutenu les raids», 2 mars 2005 http://hrw.org/french/docs/2005/03/02/darfur10230.htm
- HYCKS, V., « War Stories », Discovery Channel, 2002
- "Haïti: Nouvelle violence à Port-au-Prince", Intérêt Général, 15 octobre 2004 http://interet-general.info/article.php3?id_article=2831
- JEAN-PHILIPE, H. E., « Insécurité: le cas Préval inspire de la pitié », Haitian Promotional Group for Democracy, 5 août 2006 http://groups.yahoo.com/group/Haitianpolitics/message/45267
- KOINANGE, J., « Unspeakable brutality », CNN documentary, 23 May 2006 http://www.cnn.com/2006/WORLD/africa/05/23/koinange.rape.war/index.html
- LACOURSE, D., « Rwanda: chronique d'un génocide annoncé », Alter-Ciné, Inc., 1996
- LAVOIE, G., « Les enfants de la guerre peuvent-ils retrouver la paix? », Droit de Parole, Télé-Québec, 2001
- LETH, A. and LONCAREVIC, M., « Ghosts of Cité Soleil », Nordisk Film, 2005
- LUCAS, S., « Poursuite des kidnappings en Haïti: Nécessité de la mise en place d'une politique musclée visant à démanteler le réseau de malfaiteurs », Washington Democracy Project, juillet 2006 http://groups.yahoo.com/group/Haitianpolitics/message/45280
- MARINKER, P., « Pol Pot: Secret Killer », Biography, A&E Television Network, 1997
- MILLER, J. and SHAH, S., « Death in Gaza », Frostbite Films Productions, 2006
- MORRISON, M. and T. SANDLER, «Children of War in Northern Uganda», Dateline NBC, 22 August 2005 http://

video.msn.com/v/us/msnbc.htm?g=5000fec2-5417-42d4-b158-1566bc240f24&f=00&fg=email

- NICOLOSI, M., « Salvadoran gang said to span the nation », The Boston Globe, 28 December 2002 http://www.streetgangs.com/topics/2002/122802ms.html

- OUATTARA, M. J., « Haïti: Port-au-Prince refuse la loi des gangs », Radio France Internationale, 10 janvier 2006 http://www.rfi.fr/actufr/articles/073/article_40981.asp

- PATRY, Y., GRANA, S. and LACOURSE, L., «Hand of God, Hand of the Devil», National Film Board of Canada Production, 1996

- PERCY, N. and LYMAN, W., « The 50 Years War: Israel and the Arabs », PBS, WGBH Educational Foundation, 1999

- PROVENCHER, R., « War babies », Macumba International, Télé-Québec, 2002

- ROBINSON, S. and V. WALT, «The deadliest war in the world», Time Magazine, Vol. 167, No. 23, 5 June 2006

- RUSSO, R., « Un nouveau rôle pour l'UNHCR: protéger les personnes déplacées par la guerre civile en Ouganda », Kampala, Agence des Nations Unies pour les Réfugiés, 22 mai 2006 http://www.unhcr.fr/cgi-bin/texis/vtx/news/opendoc.htm?tbl=NEWS&page=home&id=4471d1fa4

- SHAND, T. and KEMPIN, G., « The Great War: Story of WWI, Parts I & II », Eagle Rock Entertainment, 2005

- SIBERT, C., « Face à l'opinion. Haïti: le droit à l'impunité », Cap-Haïtien, Radio Maxima, 26 mai 2006 http://groups.yahoo.com/group/Haitianpolitics/message/41654

- UNICEF, « Enfants dans la guerre et enfants-soldats », 18 mai 2004 http://www.unicef.be/campagne/fr/docs/brochure_fr.pdf

Synopsis: Children have been used since the Stone Age to fight wild beasts and hunt for food for the survival of their clans. Around 550 BC, people in positions of power have realized that children can be used as child soldiers to kill their enemies. In fact, for the last twenty years, the number of children who are used in national and international armed conflicts has increased particularly in Africa, South America, and the Middle East. However, while most of these children have been forced to join armed groups, some of them were volunteers or willingly accepted to become child soldiers who can be at a time remorseless, easily to be brainwashed, and effective killers and torturers. While international laws have always protected children as victims, should these children continue to be protected despite that they are also aggressors? If so, what about their victims who were killed, raped, or tortured? And, if those children should not be legally responsible for their crimes in international courts, is it wise for the international community to let those children be tried by their national courts, which mostly have a failing judicial system that cannot administer properly justice for juveniles or lack motivation to give justice to both victims and aggressors? In this thesis, the author is intending to set the record straight on the confusion that we see on the legal responsibility of child soldiers who are, at the same time, victims and aggressors.

Printed in the United States
by Baker & Taylor Publisher Services